*From this hill,
my hand,
Cynthiana's Wine*

resonant ⊙ publishing

resonant publishing
Baltimore, Maryland

Excerpts from J. Donald Hughes, *North American Indian Ecology*,
appear by permission (copyright © 1998 Texas Western Press)

Printed in the United States of America by
Data Reproductions Corporation, Auburn Hills, Michigan.
This book is printed on acid-free paper.

Library of Congress Catalog Card Number: 99-64945
ISBN: 0-9668716-2-6

First Edition
10 9 8 7 6 5 4 3 2 1

Cover and interior design by resonant design.
Edited by Alicia Dunphy

resonant ● publishing

Baltimore, Maryland
www.resonantgroup.com • info@resonantgroup.com

to Dorothy Weaver,
who let me start,
and to family and friends,
who keep me going

-contents-

-introduction-

THIS BOOK began as entries in a journal that I kept during the fall and winter months of 1990-'91, many years before my wife, Nadine, and I opened our small commercial farm winery, Deep Creek Cellars, in western Maryland.

Back in those days, we were among the legions of Americans making wine at home. I even made my own wine press that first year, out of oak slats liberated from a gift shop display rack that I found on the curb after the store went out of business. I guess I positioned a few of the slats a teensy bit far apart in the steel ring, so that right as a friend bent down at our big harvest party to inspect the maroon ooze flowing out between slats of the filled basket, a sopping pressurized blob of grape skins and seeds, of volleyball proportion, blew out of the basket and covered her face right around midnight.

At that hilarious instant, I decided I had to keep a diary about the glamorous craft of winemaking.

The winter of 1990-'91 was also the year I called on fruit growers in western Pennsylvania toting a certain variety of grapevine, Cynthiana, that I wanted to see grown in the area. A grape version of Johnny Appleseed, I enlisted five farmers — twenty-five plants here, fifty there — to carry out my experiment, pledging to buy all the grapes when the plants were producing. All together, we put about 200 vines in the ground.

By the end of the next year, though, I found that growers with no special interest could not be counted on to persist on my behalf. Most of the vines perished through neglect, or were eaten by deer and not replaced. I knew for certain then that I'd have to do it myself.

My wife and I worked at museums, and though we didn't make a lot of money, we did have a liberal vacation schedule and some free time. This was true more so for me than for Nadine. We had decided to wait a few years to have children, so I thought then was the moment to raise grapes.

And so, Chapter 1 begins at that point, when I planted grapes of my own on rented ground in the countryside of western Pennsylvania.

Over the months and years, as I continued writing in the journal, I grew more and more rooted in farming, an activity I knew nothing of before. I began to notice focus in my writing, having honed down the subjects observed and commented on in those crude essays to winemaking, ecology, and growing vines and other utilitarian plants, including mostly weeds; broadly, the core was a mix of "nature studies" – far away from wine – and meditations on living more tightly wound around, in, and through the natural environment.

As readers proceed here, they are asked to consider the ruthless need to limit the depth of discussion in a book that bumps up against so many subjects. This is not to say I do not address topics in depth, but rather I beg the reader's indulgence regarding my choices for extended discussion. Accordingly, I wish to say at the outset that this is more than anything a "wine" book. It ranges all over the northern hemisphere, and across immense stretches philosophically – in a sort of scholarly, or didactic way at times – but it's mostly a wine book, which I tried to keep personal and introspective while still not taking myself too seriously. Again, the reader might imagine the task.

If anything, I suspect many may find the narrative overly personal, too meditative. But this aspect shows the book to be a work which started as writings with no clear purpose for their construction. Only research and writing in the sections on midwestern wine and agricultural history were undertaken with a book in mind; otherwise, I wrote things in my journal for my own enjoyment and because I figured some of the experiences would be entertaining or useful years later. Combined with roughly four years' of additional research, in interrupted chunks stretching back to the early 1980s, the journal entries were then embellished and lengthened for this book. The reader will note direct excerpts in a couple of cases.

Once I began research in the vast literature on wine, I found a curious gap. Although a common expression among professional winemakers is, "Great wine is made in the vineyard," – probably every winemaker at every big California winery has used the expression too many times to remember – there is not one book among the hundreds in print about wine that captures the profound delights of grape-growing. There is hardly anything of an evocative nature on a subject with great potential for it. Perhaps Mark Miller's *Wine, A Gentleman's Game* (1984) comes closest, and the American Philip Wagner may certainly claim a distinguished and influential career in winegrowing and wine writing, going back to 1935. But Wagner concentrated on "how-to" guides from the perspective, primarily, of a commercial nurseryman and, like Miller, more as a winery owner than a winegrower. Certainly there are no wine books written by pure farmers (unless it's very obscure and very out of print). Wine authors over the last century, instead, are people who for a variety of reasons become recognized as authorities on a particular country or region's wines, or, forming the other main group, are columnists or correspondents in the industry's consumer or trade press. A considerable number of these authorities established their wine expertise in the wholesale and importing business, and a large percentage are British.

Because the commentators so often are salesmen, buyers, brokers, and others "in the business," wine is almost universally discussed as an upscale, mercantile, highly technical, even industrial activity. Yet, every bottle in the world starts with the tiny, fuzzy magenta, lavender, or lime green leaves that pop out on the first spring-bright day of the vintage. And so, a principal aim here is to sever the elite connotations of wine – especially in America – for let no one be kidded: wine starts in a farm field, with drippy noses wiped on longsleeves, mud caked on work fabric and human surfaces alike, and the dizziness of toil below a red sun. I do belief that if the agricultural nature and artisanal possibilities of wine are better appreciated, the beverage may be an entry-point to better living all around.

Much has been made in recent years about wine, especially red wine, being healthful, and a Danish study being publicized as I finish seems beyond a doubt to confirm the benefits of moderate wine-drinking. Yet, too many Americans consider wine a "positive" in a vacuum; I know people who "take" wine as a tonic alongside gourmet TV dinners more than once a week with atrocious levels of salt, preservatives, and fake flavorings. Others now lump wine in with "health foods" like fat-free ice cream.

Healthful living is quite a bit more complicated, but on this tangent, all I wish to say is try to find time to cook at home and relax more – and exercise. I side with my friend Isaac Bower, who says, "We need to work out less and work more."

I also hope to heighten interest in environmental considerations of how wine is grown, made, and promoted. Not a lot of agriculture can be considered "environmentally friendly," and this is certainly true with winegrowing. The industry uses a lot of chemicals, and winegrowing can be as destructive to a region's land as any other form of monoculture. Yet, there is another path for growing grapes, and an increasing number of individuals and companies are following it.

As for the environmental philosophy the reader will encounter, my purpose is to bring together popular names in American "environmentalism" – Henry Thoreau springs to mind, I hope – with less familiar, American aboriginal authorities. At the same time, I want to use the opportunity to boost my narrative at the end beyond the subject of wine. The charge will be leveled, I am sure, that I romanticize the experience of Native Americans before the white man's coming. A careful reading, however, does not support the romanticizer charge, for I tried to avoid blanket praises or condemnations, and to suggest the limits of all generalized considerations. The long excerpt from the work of a widely respected authority on Native American ecology is intended to turn the corner on my story, supplying the needed "transformative" coda of my account. My purpose was to accomplish this in the most quiet way possible, and to signify it through the tone and content of the material that follows it. I am indebted to Donald Hughes for allowing such an unusual use of his work, and I believe it brings his wisdom to a group who otherwise could never have discovered it. It is my intention that in a future book or two I can pick up where this one ends.

Those in America who agitate for a more gentle way of living in this world are always considered a fringe element, so I hope any sympathetic readers may be satisfied with the fleeting delight of seeing Thoreau, Chief Seattle, and Wendell Berry all in the same short chapter. Adjusting the ancestry of big "green" ideas in America became at some point along the way, I admit, a mission.

There is, in fact, very little new to suggest about improving the relationship between humans and the biosphere. It must be done, for our psychic if not physical survival, yet at this late date I'm afraid we're reduced to parables.

I learned long ago that when talking about oneself, keep it short. So, that was another goal. I'd been a professional journalist for nearly two decades, and hadn't found anything before worth writing a book about. Many veterans know the secret that I gained, but it's worth sharing for anyone aspiring: go do something difficult that you enjoy and express yourself about it. There's plenty left to be done in this world.

Finally, the effect of my career as editor of a regional history magazine is also apparent. Professional writing in my field requires reviews of the relevant literature in the body of the text; I think good historians make clear what is original thought and what is borrowed.

I guess I should also say what some of my goals aren't. While this is not a manual on grape-growing or winemaking, technical and how-to information is presented that is not addressed in depth in the popular literature. I hope some consider this work a primer, for surely just about any worthwhile book is partly a "how-to" guide.

Paul Roberts
November 1998
Pittsburgh, Pennsylvania

~one~

WHEN I REALIZED there was no way around it, that I would have to learn to drive the scary-awful machine myself, I did what college educates a person to do to when he's trying to learn to do most anything. He starts at the library.

"T-r-a-c-t-o-r," I punched into the computer card catalog, "h-o-w t-o."

Neither naturally nor by experience was I well-equipped mechanically. Now I'm much better, but this was 1992.

Sitting stiffly in an aluminum chair at a cool metal table in a library in Pittsburgh, where I live, I read books for two hours one afternoon about operating farm and heavy equipment. One book said most injuries occur on hillsides, when the tractor flips. Flipping is usually fatal.

Another book, probably intended originally for farm children on the Great Plains, used spritely stick figures with circle faces and red arrows to make its points. Stick arms being lopped off and stick bodies being snapped in two made the book's points easy to understand. The scowling, surprised, sad, and fearful round faces really stuck with me.

It's all in the rear wheels. Yeah, it's true, running any kind of farm implement is all in the rear wheels, if I may argue for essences in such matters. I read this at the library, though experience in the field really drove home the lesson. The downhill side wheel will become mired, and the farmer allows the uphill-side tire to keep spinning. He may not realize until too late that the spinning is going on only on one side. By then, the craft will have lost its equilibrium.

A tractor's engine is powerful, its body light. The fatal chain of events may occur in a few seconds. Flips compress time amazingly fast.

Flips're sudden.

Pay attention, warned the book; "visually check" the rear wheels if spinning or smoking rubber is heard, smelled, "or sensed." The book was saying that you can't keep looking forward, as if you're going forward, when you're spinning. Spinning in one place imperils survival. "The wise operator never fails to correct the vehicle's loss of balance."

As was often the case with reading about mechanical acts, the trip to the library left me wondering how something so difficult and dangerous ever got done. Driving a tractor seemed for all the world as perilous as steering an oceanliner.

The ground to be plowed was a steep hillside and flipping looked inevitable, I told my brother on the phone a couple of nights later.

"I want to be a wise operator. But I don't know if I can." I told him, "I'm so, I don't know, thin, and it is – GOD! – I don't know, it's so big. I just don't know . . . what am I gonna do . . . the ground must be pl –"

"Paul, Paul," my brother said, "get a hold of yourself." It was more of a shout really. He lives far away in Missouri, but he really is a constant source of inspiration by phone. "Okay, hey, you all right? What do you mean you don't know if you can do it? It's like anything else," he said. "Get on, start it up, and go forward. Just drive it.

"Hell, it can't be that hard. Farmers do it all the time."

So of course a week later I drove a John Deere-green, four-wheel drive, 600-series back and forth across the hillside all day long in Washington County, Pennsylvania, south of Pittsburgh.

I live in the southwestern corner of Pennsylvania, with my wife, Nadine. We have professional jobs in Pittsburgh, both in museums. We were in our 30s, owned a home, had no children, no outstanding VISA charges, no college debts, two older vehicles, and two younger cats.

Plowing fields was a sideline at that time. I was working the soil into flat, brown sod to plant a wine grape vineyard.

The whole thing had really started a few years earlier, also with reading, though the books weren't about anything having to do with heavy equipment. The reading was innocent and introductory, at the kitchen table; the subject was wine.

I really must add to the world's list of wonders the fact that such general information about wine, so general as to rightly be described as pre-introductory, would lead in just under ten years to the cold black seat of a John Deere 600 on a blustery cold ridge top.

And was it blustery. And scary-awful.

Well, most everybody who dares eventually realizes a dream, some dream. Ha! This turned out to be mine.

Spring 1992

INSIDIOUS IS the month of March. Its proper name should be Mudmonth. The second Saturday of March in 1992 was muddy and dank, damp, damp and cold.

Just as my brother had projected, starting the tractor and going forward pretty much all in one motion was the way to go. It was a huge machine, but moving in a straight line out of the barn wasn't too bad. Don't get me wrong, though, my mouth was very dry and my underarms very wet.

Managing the mastodon directly down the big hill to the vineyard was not too bad either (again, a straight line). But dropping the plow blades at the start of the first row that I had marked off, and watching the ground being sliced open as I inched the craft across the face of the hill was terrifying. The machine groaned and lurched as big rocks thumped and shrieked against the steel plow, broke up, and worked their way to the top of the fresh sod.

But the general fear of driving a tractor was nothing compared to the more refined terror of turning at the end of a row the first time on a steep hillside. Oh, if we could just plow straight ahead forever; but no, one must go back down a row.

Although the library book had warned that hillside turning "leads to the majority of fatalities," there was no indication one way or the other whether the horror one feels during the maneuver is an indicator of impending death. Half-way through the turn on my first try, pointed roughly downhill at an hallucinogenic angle to the clouds and earth, deep mooing and groaning erupted from the tractor's transmission (coinciding with terror mentioned above). My eyes bulged from the urge to bail out.

Then I felt the downhill tire begin to spin.

I'm sure a bomb-defuser knows such moments. Immediately I crammed the brake pedal down. In fact, I stood up on the pedal. I figured I could jump easier from a standing position. Then I recalled how the broken main stick of a figure in the book – its "back" or spine, I guess you'd say – was pictured at right angles after Farmer Stick tried to jump from a tumbling tractor.

Then I remembered to visually check the wheels. The turning of my head alerted me to sweatballs dangling above my eyes, despite the dank 35 degrees – the face, I'm sure, of a man trying to defuse a bomb. I was about to be immortalized in one of those sad three-paragraph news briefs one sees in small-town newspapers about the local farmer whose tractor turned over on a steep grade. No one saw it happen. Townspeople found him the next day.

"How could anyone be so stupid?" I mutter to myself when reading such little news briefs.

Yet, as I fought the fear, in the upright standing position, a feeling of control ironically began to spread over me. I was stopped, after all.

Checking the wheels, I found neither spinning. I was not about to flip. I was not even about to gradually, over a few minutes, like a standing-dead tree, topple over.

I took a deep breath, eased off the brake, and gave the tractor gas. The spinning began again . . . one, two, maybe three seconds. Then the giant sure-footed lizard began to claw its way back up the incline.

Not all spinning ends in death. Starting at the library to learn to drive a tractor works. Not everyone is broken in two!

Why, plowing could even be enjoyable. Confidence mounted. By the end of that silly ole cold day, I was working that hillside with a piece of straw jutting from the side of my mouth.

After busting up the sod, I used a 3-foot-long fish hook-looking imple-ment, called a subsoiler, to rip a deep furrow in the earth. Subsoil plowing shatters the strata of compacted clay typical on ridge tops of the Allegheny Mountain foothills. Grapevine roots, being rather slender as roots go, cannot penetrate "hardpan" clay, as dense as concrete and only a couple of feet underground. By breaking the soil up before planting, though, the vine's roots seek nourishment all the way down to the sandstone bedrock. Deep roots in the land anchor life.

I had to use the tractor because once I had found the land to lease, one acre about fifty minutes from my job in Pittsburgh, I had arranged for a local farmer to do the plowing. Then he neglected the task, and spring was upon me.

Plowing ground was the first of many things I learned only when forced.

Weeks later, on the 4th and 5th of April 1992, I dug 308 holes with a shovel, about 20 inches deep. And I dug the holes mostly on my knees, and planted 308 grapevines in them. Enough grapes would sprout in four or five years to make about 300 gallons of wine.

A couple of weekends later, a friend helped me put in the posts for the wire trellis which the vines grow on. Sixty posts – 8-foot sections cut from locust trees – had to be set in the ground. Sixty deep holes had to be dug. Again, the John Deere was called on. Again, the library.

Putting posts in before the plants grow tall is also among the maxims that I can confirm through experience. In what follows here, I will also try to demonstrate what effect learning from scratch a series of interrelated tasks – learning from many, and sometimes unexpected, approaches – may have on a person's well-being.

My point for the moment is to demonstrate by showing – rather than only to say it is so.

Putting in posts with a tractor involves an auger driven by the tractor's "power take-off," located usually right below the seat. The PTO, as it's called, is a turning shaft connected to the tractor's engine, and it provides the power to run many accessories.

The auger is a monster corkscrew swung into position manually behind the tractor. PTO is engaged, and a minute later a hole 25 inches deep is done. Throw the PTO into reverse and the corkscrew backs out. Eric and I slid posts into holes, shoveled and kicked dirt back in, and moved on. Each post takes less than five minutes.

Doing all of this before the plants start to send out canes is nice because the tractor rides over the plants, straddling them without harm, and the post-hole digger is easily centered in the row. Also, the tractor's big tires roll in the aisles between rows of vines, so they don't compact the loam in the plants' root zone and slow the vines' growth. The girth and heft of modern farm equipment makes soil compaction a major farming problem with many kinds of crops.

Multiply the cost of a pressure-treated, store-bought post (about $7) times sixty; it seemed a lot of money for some thick sticks. Yet there was a good alternative. In many parts of the country, people own a few acres of timber that include locust trees. I found a local guy willing to fell some of his locust trees and cut them into posts. He charged $2 per post, delivered. De-barked locust 5 to 6 inches in diameter will last thirty years, longer than hollow steel of the same size, and longer than common pressure-treated pine from the superstore "garden center." Locust is nature's fence post, with oak or walnut a poor second. Catalpa posts are best of all, if you can find them.

What's more, buying locust posts locally kept the money "in town." It didn't go off to some distant timber corporation. And in terms of resources expended, pressure-treated pine requires a lot of energy to treat and the posts are cut from inferior soft wood (usually in the South these days). A savage blight in recent years is felling locust trees in the eastern U.S. Many are standing-dead or dying, so using them is the best sort of recycling.

On top of all these reasons, one should take every opportunity to get acquainted with local residents. I contacted one farmer, for instance, who didn't have locust posts but did sell delectable honey, as well as a certain 3-foot subsoiler to lend. He even delivered.

A LOT IS WRITTEN about preparing land before planting. I know grape growers who started their vineyards twenty years ago by digging trenches in the field, then letting the land rest undisturbed over the winter. This was thought to be good. Weed seeds and roots brought to the surface during plowing died in the cold, enriching the soil with organic matter. It was said the soil "mellowed" over the winter, settling flat again on its own. But the down side is that the wind carries away topsoil and heavy winter rains cause erosion.

In recent years, a lot of good evidence has accumulated in favor of leaving the soil alone, whether the prospective plot be a field or one recently cleared of trees and brush. Then the field is planted without plowing – holes are just dug. A wise horticulturist friend of mine reasons that the farm soil in its undisturbed state is "as good as it's ever going to be." I am content merely to present the general and oft-stated preference to plow before planting. But read up before deciding. I would say that if you're going to plow ("field-dress," farmers call it), it's probably better to do it in the fall, but if you don't own land – if you're renting, as I was – such advance work often isn't possible because humans tend to make plans over the winter, at the last second.

Plowing in March or April chops up the grasses and weeds during damp spring weather ideal for germination. The soil seems stimulated, and many plants, such as the ubiquitous ragweed, regenerate best in freshly cultivated earth. In fact, the land begins a healing process, as coarse plants condition the soil for the finer grasses. If rainfall is normal, a lush summer stand of unwanted nuisance plants will result.

But obsessing about "weed control," though, isn't good. Calling any non-crop plant a "weed" pigeon-holes all as enemies, which few really are. Many common field plants have thick roots head-strong for the subsoil. Weeds in moderate quantities condition the soil by aerating it and adding fibrous matter, and they cycle nutrients from the depths, up through their stems and into their leaves. When the plants die at season's end, nutrients cycled from the subsoil enrich the topsoil. Natural succession in this process prepares the soil for grasses and wild legumes, which do not grow as rampantly as the nuisance plants. The presence of weeds in runaway populations suggests a land trying to say something – a land begging for restorative measures. Close attention, in fact, to the sorts of persistent weeds in a field can tell a farmer what minerals and nutrients are missing in the soil – a good example of how the farm is a place for art as well as plowing.

Fertilizing, or even better, sowing a cover crop of legumes and grasses in the aisles in early spring, and then turning it under in fall, is a good idea on most fields. The practice supplies nitrogen, one of the three essential farm nutrients and a building block for proteins. Fertilizing helps renew what farming rapidly depletes; typically, land used for even five years of row-crop or hay production drops to about 10 percent of its original fertility. The legume white clover makes an excellent cover crop after plowing. Besides supplying nitrogen, it spreads quickly as long as the soil is moist for germination to smother weeds, and yet it doesn't grow so tall as to require constant mowing. Most other nitrogen-fixing legumes require more maintenance. I planted the legume red clover one year, a rainy summer came along, and all I did was mow.

Other examples of legumes include trees, such as honey and black locust, which are among the first larger plants to repopulate soils in need of nitrogen. That's why you may notice these trees appearing first on stripped-off forest lands. This also explains why they are so ubiquitous on farm woodlots and along rural roads. Since white men came along, practically every inch of the countryside has been clear-cut at least a couple of times.

In farming, site decides a lot of the variables. Grapevines have been planted for centuries in soils too infertile to support other crops – on hillsides especially. Grapes make do in severe conditions, which partly explains the fascination they hold for humans and the lore grapes and wine have accumulated over the centuries.

Once the vine reaches its second year, its root system covers a large area. But in their first year, most grape plants will draw nutrients from a zone no bigger than about a 3-foot square. Some weeding in the rows among the plants, in the rich, deep soils common across much of eastern America, is logical through mid-season in each of the first two years. Young grapes need the water for themselves, but excessive weeding that exposes the soil surface directly to the sun actually reduces the moisture the grapes need, due to evaporation, even more than weed competition. This has been shown unequivocally in European research.

The more I learn, the more I seek balances. And in farming, proper balances are a moving target because no two seasons are ever the same.

For instance, tall grass in the vineyard conceals grape-loving raccoons, especially the young animals, trebling the workload of owls and hawks trying to keep the population of small scavenger mammals that eat grapes in balance. Tall grass also makes work and simple walking around aggravating. But spending two or three consecutive days in hoeing sessions under the summer sun, three or four times each summer, as I did the first two seasons – required if you don't like chemical weed-killers – leads one quickly to philosophical showdowns.

Another consideration is that one person with a full-time day job can handle only up to probably about two acres of vineyard part-time.

One of my goals is to minimize energy use by farm equipment (gasoline, oil) and wear-and-tear (on equipment and operator), though Richard Fiegel, an organic winegrower who owns Silver Thread Winery in the Finger Lakes region of New York, uses a bit more mechanization and manages (as of 1996) about six acres on his own, with a winery, full-time. "I can't imagine doing much more," he tells me, "but you can make a living with six acres – not a great living, but I'm happy enough."

I took Richard's advice to heart long ago, and the approach I eventually devised as a part-timer was the result of much reading and also of five years' of trial leading to, recently, a semblance of method. To avoid compacting my clay-rich soil, I cultivate with tillers and small garden tractors, not full-size tractors. I till, mow, and hoe. Although the mix varies with the weather of each season, in general, I: 1) cultivate the aisles in mid-May after lush spring growth, so there's lots of nutrient-rich mulch to be turned under, and then sow a cover crop of clover; 2) hoe about a 4-foot square around each grape plant in early spring, reducing competition for the vine while providing mulch nutrition, and then allow the grasses to return at their own speed during the summer, with occasional chopping, mowing and hoeing; 3) spread compost on top of the soil around the vines after leaf-fall in November. (Research shows that the nutrients, especially nitrogen, which grapevines need at the start of each growing season, come primarily from what's in the soil at the end of the previous season.) I also use a little fertilizer for each plant in each month of the growing season after fruit-set, which is usually in mid-June in my area.

Mowing rather than hoeing in the rows probably is better in wet growing seasons (as most of northeastern America's are) with vigorous grape varieties, because mature grape plants need the competition for moisture from grass and weeds to ripen the fruit. Without a killing cultivation early on, though, mowing or chopping around the plants will be pretty much a constant task.

Again, herbicides will do the work quickly – perfectly, even – but I don't see the logic, longterm, of letting soil become a holding medium for chemical eradicants. And so, I rarely use herbicides.

Plus, I don't like the brown death strips of herbicide use. And "look" – aesthetics – matters even in farming. At least it does for me.

I leave the untouched square between the hoed sections as habitat for insects both useful and beautiful such as ladybugs, praying mantises, spiders, and numerous models of tiny predatory wasps. I look forward to seeing wolf spiders, bold predators with voracious appetites, mating and raising young around my plants. Grasses in these untouched areas grow to natural field height – yes, up through the trellis wires. I cultivate some vegetable plants there, tomatoes and basil especially. Unusual primordial-looking weeds sprout, wildflowers too.

The grapes spend their days with a diverse mix of plants, animals, fungi and bacteria. The vineyard has a feral feel of good health, a walk through it always revealing something fantastical.

I do not, however, tolerate Canadian thistle. This barbed, thick-trunked hooligan hides in the grass and spikes me when I kneel to handle grape clusters or summer flowers.

THINKING ABOUT COVER CROPS and non-intensive hand- or mechanical-weeding are considerations only for people intent on "sustainable agriculture," with a general organic agenda. I didn't have such an agenda at the outset. Deciding such matters came later for me.

I first sought a place to grow grapes because I loved wine and wanted to someday either own a winery or have my own grapes for making wine at home. I suspected that my appreciation for wine would increase exponentially if I grew the grapes. That was certainly true, and in fact I think I love the farming now as least as much as the cellar work.

Reading about wine and viticulture, I was mesmerized (and still am). It's a wonderful way to learn about history, weather, geography, science, business, other cultures. Wine appreciation sharpens at least three senses (sight, smell, and taste), which makes it unique, I think, among aesthetic experiences. After that introductory night at the kitchen table, I went on to nearly all of the books on both subjects published in the United States in the twentieth century except some of the redundant instructional manuals on winemaking.

I also read many from Great Britain and Australia, the influential texts from the nineteenth century held in rare book collections, and everything translated from other languages that I could locate. For a young fellow of modest means, I maintain a fairly exhaustive collection of wine books these days, much of it dog-eared. All the reading gave me enough confidence about the basics to get started.

Then I dealt with special obstacles in the vineyard, not always successfully, by branching out to books and articles about those problems when I encountered them.

Also invaluable was my first intense practical experience. I worked a five-month harvest job in 1986 at a small California winery. And I did harvest work at other wineries elsewhere.

I used to bore people cross-eyed talking about wine at social gatherings. (Many would argue I still do.) My victims become ensnared after asking the innocent question, "How did you get started at this?"

One Saturday in December 1991, driving on U.S. 40 in Washington County, Pennsylvania, I came to Scenery Hill. The hamlet with the oldest operating restaurant and tavern in America west of the Allegheny Mountains straddles the road for about 300 yards on a picturesque ridge top, 1,400 feet above sea level. The leaves were gone from the trees, so back off the highway I could see rows of an orchard perched on the lip of the ridge, facing south. My search for a south-facing hillside began after reading they are positioned best to catch the sun during critical early growth in spring and during ripening days in autumn. Famous vineyards in northerly growing districts – Burgundy, for instance, in France – face mainly south.

I also read that the ideal location for a hillside vineyard was about two-thirds of the way up a steep hill. Cold air is heavier and flows to lower ground, while the very top of a hill may stay a couple of degrees colder than the sides, because of the extra altitude.

I studied weather data, too. Washington County winters are much colder than Burgundy's, but their climates during the growing season are similar, with quite a few cloudy days, summer rainstorms, and persistent but not oppressive humidity. (A visit in 1994 to Burgundy would confirm similarities in topography, too.) Furthermore, Washington County was a big producer of apples and peaches in the nineteenth century. Apples will grow farther north, but "where the peach excels," one manual from the 1880s enthuses, "plant the grape."

From the road off the highway, I inspected the acres of apple trees, and then found the lane leading to a wooden farmhouse in need of repairs and paint. Coal smoke curled from the chimney. When I knocked, Dorothy Weaver, 77, appeared.

"Well, I don't see any reason you couldn't plant some grapes here," said Mrs. Weaver after I explained my visit. She invited me in, and I learned that she owned about 110 acres, with about twenty acres in fruit trees.

"How long do your grapes take for fruit?" she asked. "How many years?"

"I think three years, though if things go right maybe just two."

When I came back from looking around her farm, I asked if I could rent a section of a hillside about two-thirds of the way up one of her southwest-facing hills, and a second small area over the hill facing due east.

Mrs. Weaver was kind and generous to me. Her husband once had operated a successful orchard at the farm for some thirty years. He grew apples, peaches and a few plums. People in Scenery Hill have told me that regular customers came from 100 miles away, as far as central West Virginia, for the Weavers' Golden and Red Delicious apples.

Mrs. Weaver died in 1995, and her youngest son then operated the orchard, to a much diminished extent for another year. Then the property was sold at auction, and I have continued to lease the land from the new owner.

One of the last things Mrs. Weaver's husband, Don, had done before his death in 1988 was buy a John Deere 600-series tractor.

I at first feared many other things besides the tractors, mostly because of what I didn't know. A lot of years had passed since I had been exposed to work country-style. That's because the shovel and spade of construction jobs in the small town where I grew up had made me swear that I'd earn a living with my brain, not my back.

By the time I was a grown-up and doing the things that adults do, and had enough money to buy property, I was married and we were working in Pittsburgh. So we bought a city house. I became a city dweller and worker. I sat in a chair a lot. The sitting got to me; my back hurt. The job also had its share of stress, which I slowly became aware of feeling in my abdominal tract – only at the end of the day for a while, but much more often later. This was distressing and sometimes painful.

I also started to notice that every morning in the summer, with the windows open, I woke up to a smell of something burning in the bedroom – car exhaust from the expressway a mile away.

Certainly I used my brain in the city: in a stimulating job, in constant conversation, at provocative lunches and happy-hours, at films and plays and poetry readings and music shows, at bars, exhibit openings, museums, coffeehouses, dinner and house parties by the dozen – at all the activities and opportunities the city offers, I used my brain. My head, it seemed, could not complain.

For a few years – five, actually – I was contented. I had never lived in a city before coming to Pittsburgh in 1987, and the "urban life" marketed in the entertainment sections of the newspaper and the hip weekly "city papers" was alluring. Then I began to realize how often I went to bed mentally taxed, and yet, because I'd had so little physical exertion during the day, was so twitchy that I couldn't fall asleep. There was a lot of movement for sure, a frenzy of movement, but how strange it was to move around all day and still be exhausted mainly in the head.

I am not saying that others do not experience what I felt, or that I felt them more profoundly; indeed, I am describing almost stereotypical pressures of urban living. Neither do I claim to be a casualty or a burn-out from life in the fast lane. Pittsburgh, believe me, is not that fast. But I did conclude that I should look for a better balance between the life of the mind in town and and a life with time in the country.

I am not saying it is the decision for everyone, but that it was for me is certain.

The Oglala Sioux Luther Standing Bear has written that "man's heart, away from nature, becomes hard." I believe Standing Bear. I didn't know of him or his "ways" in 1992. What difference it makes is really what this account is all about – that, and why I decided that ultimately I'd rather live in the country and visit the city, rather than the other way around. Even this I had to learn from scratch.

A concise chronology is that in the summer of 1996, after four years of growing grapes at Scenery Hill, and two years of searching for land and debating how to run a winery and still commute to jobs in the city, my wife and I bought property well beyond commuting distance. Our land is in western Maryland, one hour and forty-seven minutes in good traffic from our house, and fifty minutes east of Scenery Hill, in the mountain chain that straddles the Pennsylvania-Maryland border.

We kept our jobs in Pittsburgh, and in the spring of 1997, built a small winery into the side of a hill on vacation time and weekends, and planted more grapes on our own south-facing hill above the winery. In the fall of 1997, we used more vacation time and weekends to bring in grapes from California and several eastern growers, supplementing our Scenery Hill supply, and made our first commercial wines. In coming vintages, we will rely more and more on our vineyards, and also more on farm products besides wine.

I hope one day soon to be completely weaned of city living. I think by then I may look forward to the occasional exhibit openings or art films, and the rush of humanity.

GROWING UP, I was deathly afraid of spiders. But the first time that I bent over to plant a vine at Scenery Hill, two hairy hockey puck-sized wolf spiders hopped up out of the soil and ran across my hands. I sprang to my feet in the middle of the field, shivering, only to look around and see that the plowed turf in all directions was alive with wolf spiders. The sun glinted off their silvery crawling hairs. It was their mating season; plowing had disturbed the spiders in their burrows.

I had not seen a single one before. Not until I got down into the soil had I seen anything.

Growing grapes wasn't along any straight line that I could have plotted to any final goal. One of the great unexpected joys of the ensuing six years was spending so much time outdoors. If I hadn't planted grapes, my time outdoors would have been much less, and what came into my head and heart would have been less satisfying. I know more, yet am aware as never before of mysteries.

But that is to jump way ahead.

My fascination with wine is where the narrative properly begins, and the fascination was a decade in the making before I shoveled dirt from a single hole. I decided to plant in 1992 mainly because the grape variety that I thought would make a distinctive and tasty red wine wasn't being grown in Pennsylvania. I was forced to do it.

-*two*-

WHAT GOT ME INTERESTED in wine, going on twenty years ago, was a red from the Bordeaux region of France. Quite a few wine lovers report conversion by red Bordeaux, and mine was Chateau La Lagune from 1970, a fabulous vintage, which was poured on my behalf at a birthday dinner in 1983. The La Lagune, just then maturing, sticks in my mind the way a favorite old song does for some people. It had a very distinctive smell of fresh mulberries plus, of course, the usual great Bordeaux melangé of other things like roasted nuts, leather, and violets. I can still taste it, too, though above smell or even taste, what I remember best is its texture, its feel in the mouth: old-fashioned generosity, smooth as warm butter, at once rustic and refined. Texture is the fabric of life, and so it goes with wine; the La Lagune slumped against the curve of the goblet, looking nearly alive. As I've come to know wine better, and how to make it, I've learned that making wine with a nice smell and flavor is fairly easy, but giving it real life, a feel in the mouth the evokes all of life's nuance and complexity, is a higher calling that few consumers or winemakers value.

Since my introduction to the beverage during, yes, high school – Boone's Farm Strawberry Hill, in the woods behind the grade school – I'd had no association with any wines but the cheap and sweet, and so after tasting the first ounce of La Lagune, I simply could not believe what my senses told me. By the end of dinner, I was awestruck: how, I wondered, could human beings and nature conspire to make something so ravishing?

It is said that the enjoyment of fine dry wines usually is an acquired taste, but not so with me. I took to that mulberry fruit like mother's milk.

I also took instantly to the mythical persuasion of the grape transformed.

I began drinking wine most every evening at dinner and, in those first few decadent weeks, after meals long into the night. I think it was my good fortune to learn about wine so intensely in the company of food. Today, dinner without a glass of wine . . . well, it just isn't a meal.

I could expostulate for pages about the health benefits of wine – why, it's practically a health tonic – but the mass media have already done a pretty good job of that in recent years. Hardly a week passes without a report of a new health study finding in favor of wine. I wish only to add something about the texture of gracious living: I have noticed over the years that people who drink wine regularly at mealtime don't imbibe much during the rest of the day, and that the full formula for healthfulness includes doing most everything else in moderation. Like eating meat, for instance. I profess pure adoration for lamb shanks, cooked slowly till the flesh may be eaten with a spoon, but six out of seven days vegetable entrees satisfy just fine. Wine is also "people-oriented," best enjoyed with friends and family, and it is that combination which tends to temper the human craving for excess in thought as in deed.

The most endearing feature of wine appreciation is what one learns "on the side." As I said earlier, studying winemaking and winegrowing is a wonderful way to learn on the side. I've picked up lessons about the economy and history, for example, of southwestern France. The most popular grape there is Carignan; in fact, it's the most widely planted red wine grape in the world, and one I use at my own winery because I love its sinewy texture and its artisanal associations.

Carignan is actually an immigrant to France, having migrated in the 14th century from neighboring Catalonia in Spain. Bullfights are still held in this region of France, and the Catalan language is widely spoken.

The region as a whole is known to the French public as the Midi, and for more than a century was the source of factory worker reds. Few "fine" wines were made, and as recently as ten years ago, even in one of its celebrated districts, Rousillon, less than twenty of the roughly 150 wine estates bottled their own wines. Unlike in America, large cooperatives do most of the winemaking and nearly all of the bottling. (U.S. consumers can most easily meet the winemakers in bottles labeled "Corbieres" or "Coteaux du Provence.") Wine literally runs in the blood of the Midi, an area the size of

Texas and New Mexico combined where some 5,000 individual landowners cultivate grapes. It is, writes one authority, Rosemary George, "full of contrasts and contradictions," possessing an ancient devotion to the grape while also being "the vineyard of the future, for the potential is tremendous."

As an American with what seems an obsession with wine, I still cannot claim to know personally 50 individuals engaged in winegrowing. And so for me, there is guaranteed fascination. To consider the craft's influence in the culture of southwestern France, during six centuries in but one of the Old World's great wine regions, is truly a source of continual amazement. It's why I never tire of learning about wine, and why I look most to Europe for wine insights and direction.

Returning to our own shores, in our own earlier times, six weeks or so after I tasted that La Lagune back in the early '80s I sampled a dry red made from an unusual grape variety bred in my native state of Missouri. A 1981 from Stone Hill Winery, it was rich and intensely flavored, and oozing with unusual coffee and berry smells. Wow! What nerve! I eyed the wine in that glass the way one contemplates a heckler.

With the source so near – an hour from where I lived in Columbia, Missouri – my headlong dive into the wine world was conveniently localized. The Show-Me State has more than 40 wineries, and I ventured out with passion to see them. After stops at modest tasting rooms, I would trek to their vineyards, which more often than not were located right behind the tasting room. I met the pruners, the grass-cutters, the fungicide sprayers, and the winemakers, who more often than not were first spied sweating and breathless, running from vineyard to tasting room to greet customers.

These experiences, too, were good fortune, for I learned about wine firsthand and by seeing the clear connection between winegrowing and the bottled product. I also saw what a tenuous existence it was for many owners.

Crucial to my endeavors was Larry Carver, whose winery 90 miles south of Columbia near Rolla, Missouri, was pretty much a classic of the type. He made excellent dry wines, and worked himself half to death doing it. Forced to rely on the rare worldly sort who happened past his sign on U.S. 63, his winery barely survived and the Carvers lived from one month to the next (closing in 1988).

I walked into Larry's tasting room one Saturday in 1983, and within a month, after constant weekend visits, was recruited – that is, made such a nuisance of myself that Larry had to do something with me – to help with oddball chores around the winery.

The first task was planting. "Can you dig holes?" he asked, "about 'yea' deep" – indicating 18 inches on the shovel stock – "and 'yea' wide" – again measured on the shovel handle – "then put the plant in and cover it up with soil? Being a winemaker is awfully exact, huh?"

We became friends over several summer weekends. In exchange, I got to taste a lot of wine. He was about 50, and I was exactly 25, and he remained patient with my youthful enthusiasms. "Anyone who likes red Bordeaux straight out of the blocks is worth listening to," he merrily told his wife, whose scowl greeted me before 8 a.m. one Saturday when she opened the front door to find me loitering outside.

"You finally ready to get going?" Larry joked to me, sloshing black coffee on his wife's house robe as he brushed past.

My early hands-on education still reverberated nine years later, when I planted the grape variety in western Pennsylvania that had made Stone Hill's wine, and that also had made the luscious stuff I talked Larry out of filtering to sterility that summer at Carver Wine Cellars (a wine I still vividly recall: black as a moonless night, with the pungency of blueberry liqueur; how I loved it unfiltered!). The grape variety responsible for those libations was Cynthiana.

At this point, it seems only fair to prepare the reader for the full measure of my spasms for Cynthiana, and the complete explanation set to follow. With excellent primary sources available in the Special Collections Library at the University of Missouri-Columbia, I took to researching the grape and its history. I spent dozens of hours reading about the early years of cultivating Cynthiana in Missouri and the Midwest, and learned that a particular group of nineteenth-century German immigrants were the principal growers.

The links to the present-day, plus being able to grow and taste the very wine that they had pioneered, captured my imagination and embroiled me in the culture of wine to an extreme and distinctive degree.

In what follows, a lot of wine is to be served with travel across numerous states and even another continent, along with quite a bit of history (occasionally personal, but mostly not). My meanderings will stray far from wine and farming but will return, I promise – especially to farming and to Cynthiana's wine.

A VIAL-FULL OF BOTANY. There are about fifty species of grapes in the world, but nature has engineered only ten or so species to contain enough natural sweetness to be suitable for wine. (Complex sugar chains, sucrose and fructose mainly, are converted to alcohol during fermentation.) Cynthiana, it so happens, is a representative of one of those good species, *vitis aestivalis*.

Probably the species known best is native not to North America, as is Cynthiana, but rather to Europe. Pre-Christians of southern Eurasia were the first to bring *vitis vinifera* from the wilds into cultivation, and by the time of the Roman empire, viniculture was well-established in Europe.

Cabernet Sauvignon, the modern world's most sought-after red wine grape, is thought by some to be one of the oldest varieties in cultivation. A few historians hold that Cabernet is related to the ancient grape which the Greek agriculturist Pliny called Biturica, while others trace its lineage only to the early 1700s, to the Vidure variety in Bordeaux. As is true of many of the acceptably good varieties (Spain's Tempranillo, Italy's Sangiovese, eastern Europe's Kadarka, for instance) and the "noble" varieties (Cabernet, Chardonnay, Pinot Noir, Riesling), people have different stories to explain a grape's popularity.

Cabernet Sauvignon, Pinot Noir, Chardonnay, and Zinfandel, all *vinifera* and all popular varietal labels on wine bottles in the United States, are but a small fraction of the European varieties now distributed throughout the world's vineyard lands. In France alone, perhaps as many as thirty or forty *vinifera* varieties – Poulsard, Trousseau, Malbec, Mourvèdre, on and on – exhibit particular advantages, whether in the vineyard or in the cellar, that make them important in one or more of France's twenty or so major wine producing areas. Italy, too, has numerous oddball grapes of regional importance. Switzerland's principal white grape, Chasselas, makes forlornly mediocre wine everywhere else it is grown. Germany, Spain, Portugal, Greece, the countries of the former Yugoslavia and the Soviet Union, and the old Soviet "eastern bloc" neighbors all have countless *vinifera* grapes beloved, or just tolerated, almost exclusively by provincial winemakers. For a grape to be carried far from its home, as Cabernet has been is the exception rather than the rule.

Knowledge, equipment, and human resources marshaled to grow grapes often varies with the variety: like people, grape plants are of different character, with distinct habits and needs. Some varieties must be fussed over, others grow with few cares. Even plants of the same variety within a vineyard may possess a singular personality: one grows more profusely (or vigorously, as growers say), sets more fruit, or needs more water and nutrients than an "identical" plant beside it. And quite distinct from the know-how needed to grow grapes is the knowledge useful for turning them into wine, though of course the two worlds are complementary. They are endlessly fascinating worlds, as well, because wine made from a particular variety grown in Algeria is likely to bear little resemblance, besides its color, to wine from that variety tended in New York or Chile or Bulgaria.

More than two dozen grapevine species are native to North America. Cynthiana is an odd case. Whether it is a cross between *aestivalis* and another species (some experts suspect a cross with *vinifera*), or it is a wild grape, a pure *aestivalis*, is simply not known. And no apparent way exists to resolve the question. *Aestivalis* and its natural variants, or sub-species, are common along the edges of lowland forests across a large part of eastern, southern, and central North America. Early works on American horticulture, such as Philadelphian John Bartram's in the 1770s, describe what we may conclude today was *aestivalis*. In his travels through hill and valley in the Mid-Atlantic region of the early colonies, he reports residents' preference for a small but highly flavored wild black grape especially suited, it was said, for winemaking. The type was well enough known to be gathered already by a nickname: "summer grape." (Later scientific classifications would build on that moniker by assigning the species its Latin description "*aestival*: of or relating to summer.")

Fruit hybridizers (a briefing on the crossing of native varieties by amateur botanists appears later in this account) concentrated on this common species in the early nineteenth century, so that Cynthiana as a named variety was first offered for sale commercially in 1830. By American standards, this makes it an ancient; in fact, it may well be the oldest native grape now in wide cultivation. This modern chapter in Cynthiana's story, of which much more will follow, is now unfolding before a growing and wildly appreciative audience in eastern America. At this point, perhaps a few thousand people have heard of the grape and enjoyed its wine. Many authorities, however, believe its day is on the horizon as the most popular non-*vinifera* variety for reliably good red table wines east of the Rockies.

Summer 1992

THE LIVING LABORATORY that was my first season of growing the grapevine, the heralded if still largely unknown Cynthiana, yielded more perspiration and isolation than any illuminations about the secret of fine wines. Very early on, certainly by Memorial Day 1992, I worried that I'd bitten off more than I could chew.

That sixty-minute drive frequently took more like ninety during the evening rush hour out of Pittsburgh. Intent upon giving the vines a solid headstart on the weeds, I felt called upon to endure the jammed commuter routes at least a couple of times a week at the start so I could combat all competing vegetation in the rows as soon as it appeared.

I learned the hard way that the space between rows depends largely on the equipment to be used to maintain the vineyard. Ten feet seemed like a nice round number to me, so I had asked Jack, Mrs. Weaver's one son who had agreed to share maintenance duties, and he had said that 10 feet sounded fine to him. (I should have known better, for he was the son who had promised to plow the ground but never did it.) So, I discovered after planting that the grass-cutting attachment on the Weaver's tractor was 9 feet wide.

Try mowing in a line that can vary only 1 foot over the length of a 190-foot row: there is no way without veering off course and taking out vines.

A neighbor, Dennis Sweeney, had a smaller tractor with a rotary tiller, so I hired him to till the rows in mid-June. That worked well, but hiring his services a few times each summer would get expensive.

"Heard you had Dennie doing some work," said Mrs. Weaver the Saturday after, when I stopped at her house to say hello on my way to the vineyard. She snickered when I confirmed the rumor. "Lou was saying that all you was doing was planting weeds," she added.

Her son Lou, a Vietnam vet who was nothing but surly to me, had moved back to the area from Florida and gradually was taking over for Jack in operating the farm. He considered me a bumpkin, I could tell, and probably also wondered if I had designs on buying the property from his mother.

I considered her comment, and wondered, for the first time, if Jack had intentionally misled me about the width of the tractor implement.

"Well, Lou's comment would be real comical, Mrs. Weaver, except it was your other son who told me 10-feet when your grass cutter is a full 9," I said. "Now your mower won't fit between the rows. And I can't un-plant the vines."

"Well, just planting weeds is all you're doing," was her reply.

Money spent on gasoline getting back and forth from the city also weighed heavily in those early estimates of the eventual commercial value of so small a planting. And there was little competition for the depressing calculations once I arrived at the vineyard, since I often spent the remainder of the workday evening or an entire Saturday without seeing a soul.

From the Weaver's hill, no houses are within sight when the leaves are on in the summer. It was gorgeous, but the quiet and contrast to the high-speed traffic on the way took some getting used to. I realized finally how silence could be deafening. Any "action" was all natural. Even a turkey vulture's circlings were soundless.

There was also plenty of rain and I quickly found out that I needed a lawnmower to cut the grass, since Lou, though he had a riding mower, refused to use it on my plot. "Your agreement was with Jack, not me," he huffed.

I wasn't about to spend big money on a new mower, only to learn it was another wrong choice, so I bought a $50 Briggs & Stratton out of the newspaper classifieds. Starting cheap and small and working up in size slowly, I could see, was the way to go.

The grapes, by contrast, were happy to grow in leaps. Once I measured a vine shoot when I arrived on a Saturday morning and found when I measured it again before leaving that evening that it grew a quarter of an inch in one day.

The grass-cutting and weeding of June became July's, which gave way to the humidity of August and the late summer hush of early September. By then, most of the vines were 3 feet tall. Except during a couple of weeks at the ocean on vacation, I never missed a weekend of tying the shoots, copiously, to the 3-foot-tall stakes which kept the vine's limbs up off the ground so I could mow around them.

Pre-cut stakes from the lumberyard would have cost $1 each, so I used the method I'd seen in wine books of Italy – broken tree limbs, gnarled and irregular, and splintered boards or other wooden shards, salvaged from country woodlot and urban curbside alike. My plot looked like it was owned by a junkyard man who wouldn't tolerate weeds.

By early October, vine leaves were red and gold and falling. It frosted October 21st, according to my extensive notes from that year. Except to prepare for Year 2, that was that for Year 1.

ONE OF THE MOST OBVIOUS facts I learned during the 1980s in my introduction to wine from eastern America is that no native grapes besides Cynthiana make superior table wines. The reason is a set of chemical flavor and aroma constituents which in the trade are called "foxyness;" sometimes the character is a cloying, bubble-gum smell and taste, and sometimes it's more like wild strawberries. A half-dozen or so commercial varieties of native American ancestry are grown in a broad swath from western Kansas to eastern Virginia, and many wineries turn the odd fruit cocktail foxyness to their advantage in sweet wines, where such characteristics are tolerable. Many people, in fact, enjoy the "American" flavor. Concord jelly, for example, has it in spades.

Only native American grapes possess this peculiar property, but for some reason Cynthiana wines have none of the foxyness that mars dry wines from other native varieties. It does have an intensely "grapy" flavor which, to me, does call to mind Concord jelly. There's even a hint of elderberries in Cynthiana's flavor, especially when the wine is young.

Using this unusual dimension – after all, grapyness is pretty much ideal for purposes of making grape wine – vintners in a few states are making wines today of world-class value from Cynthiana. Missouri leads the pack, both historically and in recent years. Until very recently, though, few wine drinkers knew, for word had not gotten beyond the fairly small cluster of midwesterners who enjoy dry native table wines.

But before getting into what wine drinkers and wine experts think about Cynthiana wines today, an historical detour, a sort of ampelographical flash-back, should prove titillating. What came before, in Cynthiana's "other life," endured for longer than its current resurgence can so far claim. So, it should not be glossed over.

MISSOURI AND VIRGINIA wineries were known internationally in the middle part of the nineteenth century for wines from Cynthiana. I know, I know. A second reading of the sentence may be needed.

As was the case with Cabernet Sauvignon, Cynthiana, or a grape nearly identical to it, went by other names – Norton, or Virginia Seedling, or even Norton's Virginia Seedling. The center of the "Virginia claret" region, pro-ducing wines labeled Virginia Seedling or Norton, was the southwestern part of the state near Charlottesville (a half-century after the untimely death of a grape promoter who split his time about equally between governance and gastronomy – Thomas Jefferson).

In Missouri, fine wines came from the central, eastern, and southwestern sections. In 1873, a Cynthiana made just south of St. Louis was declared the "best red wine of all nations" at a worldwide competition in Vienna. The following year, a French commission studying American wines at Montpellier gave Missouri's Cynthiana wines the same high marks.

Taking into account the awful hyperbole that rises like vapor from wine competitions, then as now, one must be impressed by the more measured remarks of Henry Vizetelly, a Londoner of first-rank significance in nine-teenth century wine commentary. Vizetelly, upon tasting the award-winner at the 1873 Vienna Exposition, declared it "full-bodied, deep-coloured, and aromatic," before slyly adding, "only needing finesse to equal a first-rate Burgundy."

I always like to know what sort of wine was made in times past from varieties we know today. Nineteenth century Burgundy wines were different than its wines of modern reputation. They typically were powerful, rough-edged country drinks without the roundness for which Bordeaux reds, for instance, were building a reputation by mid-century. So, although some Cynthiana practitioners admitted a predilection for water as a blending and thinning agent, its earliest wines probably were not so different than the dark and dense barrel-aged style in vogue today.

Ironically, this is Bordeaux's modern reputation, and it is Bordeaux, not Burgundy, that the majority of American winemakers, especially in eastern America, use as a benchmark for their finest reds. In America, only in the last half-generation has wine competed with bourbon and beer as a national drink. For that and other reasons, America's most beloved wines are full-bodied and strong. Bravado seems contagious, or at least an easy trait to copy.

Among those who knew early Cynthiana wines well was the midwestern politician and essayist Friederich Muench. He stated shortly after the Civil War that Cynthiana's wine, when "two or three years old, cannot be excelled by the best red wines of the old world." Missouri and Virginia vintages were stocked in many of the nation's finest hotels and restaurants. The wine was traded in probably two dozen states. President U.S. Grant is known to have kept a righteous supply in his White House cellars.

Missouri, by 1870, ranked third among the states in wine production, with semi-sweet wines from the native Catawba and other whites leading the list.

But it was Cynthiana which distinguished Missouri from the pack. Philanthropist and writer Charles Loring Brace, stopping over in 1867 fresh from a wine-tasting expedition in California, concluded that "no red wine has ever been produced in America equal" to a Missouri Norton.

Years later, in 1908, the author of the most exhaustive study of grape varieties published in the United States would state that Norton "is the leading wine grape in eastern America" and "the wine made from it is the best of its class."

All of this is high praise for Missouri's wine industry, yet probably not one regular wine-drinker in a thousand knows of the Show-Me State's astonishing legacy.

The grape was tried but did not bear well in California conditions, but thrived as far north as Bass Island in Lake Erie off the Ohio shore, and east to New York and New Jersey. (A few dozen old Cynthiana vines still exist in New Jersey vineyards, in fact.)

Between 1850 and 1900, producers in a dozen mostly southern and midwestern states reported nothing but success with the grape. It was also grown in France, certainly on a small scale, for at least two decades in the late nineteenth century.

Such widespread success for a native grape selected from hundreds of other natives tried and discarded in the 1800s persuaded Liberty Hyde Bailey, in his monumental *The Evolution of Our Native Fruits* (1906), to call Norton an "epoch-making grape."

Later in the century, after epochral changes in the nation's economic system and Prohibition had wiped out grape-growing in nearly every state but California, Frank Schoonmaker and Tom Marvel (*American Wines*, 1941), reported that in Virginia, "it is this Norton wine . . . for which the public is waiting." A member of a fledgling wine cooperative near Charlottesville, later to fail for untold reasons, told the authors: "It is the Norton grape upon which [its] members" were concentrating.

Baltimore newspaper editor Philip Wagner, who began publishing books on wine in the mid-1930s and still ranks as the most prolific figure in twentieth century U.S. wine literature, declared his appreciation for the variety in successive editions of his books.

In *A Wine-Grower's Guide* (1965), Wagner describes Cynthiana wine as having "intense color, and a distinct" bouquet. He had tasted dozens of wines made from the grape. In 1991, I interviewed Wagner, who was the man most responsible for introducing North America to another sort of grape, the French-American hybrids which now dominate eastern winemaking. "Cynthiana is clearly the best American grape," he said. "It makes a truly distinctive wine, a real American specialty, and with all the 'yackety-yack' about Cabernet and Chardonnay – you'd think there were only two grapes in the world – it's a shame that more people don't know more about about it."

In successive editions of *The Wines of America*, author Leon Adams praises Cynthiana and Norton, agreeing with Wagner that they are (3rd edition,

1985) the "best of all native American red-wine grapes."

I interviewed Adams in 1986 at his home in Sausalito, California. "I really think Cynthiana wines are first-rate," he said. "When I was traveling in Missouri and Arkansas doing the research for my third edition, I was thrilled to find those wines."

One of the earliest producers to make headlines outside its home state was Cowie Cellars, near Altus, Arkansas. "That wine had the essence of strawberries – delicious," recalled Adams between sips of a Contra Costa County Zinfandel he served during my visit. Then he looked at his glass and said: "Completely different than this wine – much lighter, but delicious; the sort of wine not many American winemakers know how to make."

Robert Cowie's wine had sneaked in among what was otherwise a California landslide at a major eastern wine competition in 1984. Adams related how he had told Cowie shortly after the winemaker had received his silver medal his was "world-class caliber – certainly the finest dry red wine between the two oceans."

It was Cowie's wine, Adams and I concurred that day in Sausalito, that really showed the possibilities for the grape. I, too, had tasted the wine, having driven for six hours once to Altus from Columbia for a few bottles; unlike most Cynthiana wines, Cowie's was light in body and, yes, it evoked beautiful sweet strawberries.

Another admirer is Lucie Morton. In *Winegrowing in Eastern America* (1986), she rates Norton as having the "best potential for cellar-aged wines made from pure native American grapes." Morton has a little planted at her family's farm in Virginia. "We make a good wine with it for ourselves," the renowned winegrowing consultant told me a few years ago. "I travel a lot, and what I like about the vine is you can go away for weeks at a time and when you come back it'll be fine. It'll take a lot of neglect."

Barbara Ensrud (*American Vineyards*, 1988) calls a Norton from Stone Hill Winery "reminiscent of Bordeaux," but with a taste "all its own . . . a solid, meaty wine that can easily stand with some of the world's better reds."

But perhaps the biggest modern break for Cynthiana came in 1993, when *Gourmet* wine columnist Gerald Asher devoted his April feature to a review of Missouri's industry, emphasizing an "indigenous grape that might yet do for Missouri what Cabernet Sauvignon has done for California." His was the first really substantive discussion of Cynthiana in a national periodical in more than a century. Lavished with five older vintages from Stone Hill's cellars in Hermann, Missouri, Asher wrote: "I was astonished to find the wines so remarkably good. They were more meaty than fruity, with something of the Rhone about them. The 1985, in particular, rounded out by its time in wood and fully developed by several years in the bottle, was quite delicious.

"I finally understood, as I never really had before, why Vizetelly had been so confident of Missouri's wine future."

Since Asher's column, Norton wines made near Charlottesville, Virginia, have attracted national attention again. Horton Vineyards' 1992 Norton, blended with 20 percent Mourvèdre also grown at the estate, received rave reviews from *Washington Post* wine critics upon it release in Summer 1994. The wine sold well in D.C. and Virginia stores for about $9.

Horton opened a new epoch for the grape when its wine went on sale shortly before Thanksgiving 1994 in Massachusetts – the first wine from this variety sold commercially outside its region in perhaps one hundred years. Horton's Norton is now even more widely available. Not surprisingly, Horton's label plays up the wine's historical roots in Virginia.

EXCEPT TO THOSE INTENSELY interested in wine, the superlatives may not mean much. But to put the remarkable story of the Cynthiana grape into perspective is to see it as an American classic. The wine has made a fabled journey from wild popularity to obscurity and back that is not so different than, say, Levi's 501 denim jeans. The grape is not known to most wine consumers because the U.S. wine press has a tendency to bang the drum loudest about established favorites such as Cabernet Sauvignon and Chardonnay. Excellent wines of regional importance are very few in America, so the mainstream wine press may be excused for not picking up on the only American grape capable of producing a decent red table wine.

Most recent developments suggest that the press and the retail trade are in the early stages of accepting Cynthiana wines, and are beginning to position them in the dizzying galaxy of competitors in retail stores. In late 1994, perhaps following Asher's lead, the *Wine Enthusiast* enthusiastically placed the '92 Horton, with its vibrant smoky fruit, in a list of "Rhone-like" U.S. blends; all the other entries were Californian.

"Which was great," said Owen Smith. "That's right where we want to be, with all the interest in Rhone-type wines." (Smith told me this while he was the winemaker at Horton; he's now at California's R.H. Phillips Winery.)

Released in May 1994, the '92 Horton Norton sold out in early 1995. "It's just amazing how that wine did," said Smith. "We started from scratch, with very little modern-day name recognition for the grape, and it really blew out the door."

Smith believes the Rhone reference is appropriate. "Norton and Mourvèdre definitely have this weird symbiotic thing. We don't know what it is, but it's there." Mourvèdre is of ancient Spanish origin but is grown most successfully in southern France, reaching its apogee in the long-lived reds of the Bandol appellation. Like California, where a few dozen acres' worth find their way into blends by wineries such as Bonny Doon and R.H. Phillips, Virginia has the heat to ripen it.

Dennis Horton's winery turned out 1,000 cases of the Norton-Mourvèdre blend in '92 and 2,300 cases in 1993 from his 8 acres of Norton vines. The winery crushed 40 tons of Norton in 1994, 20 percent more than the year before; this meant the vineyard was producing a very respectable 5 tons per acre, which should satisfy growers who are hesitant to plant untried varieties for fear they won't produce enough fruit to be financially worthwhile. The winery also offers a blend of 40 percent Mourvèdre with equal parts of Cabernet Franc and Norton for about $9.

In Missouri, Cynthiana wines are sold in grocery stores and 7-Elevens, as well as specialty wine stores. Missouri is the unchallenged king of Cynthiana, but its remote position far from the coastal wine centers and the wine press has meant that thirty-five years of Cynthiana production has gone practically unnoticed beyond the state's borders.

Except to a tiny group of committed afficianados, that is. Stone Hill, the state's oldest and most successful winery, turns out about 4,300 cases of Bordeaux-styled Norton each year (as of 1997), and aims to crush 120 tons of its own Norton grapes by the end of the decade. For at least fifteen years,

Stone Hill's Norton has had a big, mainly midwestern cult following; every deep purple drop of every vintage sells out at prices that in recent years have cleared $20 a bottle. Stone Hill lately has added an "Old Vine Reserve," from Civil War-era vines on its property, which goes to only the truly annointed.

At last count, ten Missouri wineries were trying their hand at the grape, most as premium, barrel-aged wines above $15. Three wineries in Arkansas offer the wine. (Appendix IV is a list of all the wineries in every state where Cynthiana is produced.) For anyone counting, Cynthiana wines have won barrelfuls of medals in state wine competitions in the last two decades, and many have taken awards in national contests since 1990. Two central West Virginia growers recently planted Cynthiana, untried in the region since Prohibition, and their first wines are just now emerging. One of the growers, Alan Wolfe, owner of Jones Cabin Run Vineyards and a consultant to several West Virginia wineries, matter-of-factly predicts that "Norton is going to be the bread-and-butter red wine grape in the East in twenty years."

Interest in Missouri has reached something approaching a fever pitch; by 1993, plantings of Cynthiana outstripped other varieties 3-to-1. The state has some 300 acres devoted to it, with hundreds more planned by 2000.

At least three commercial nurseries sell rooted Cynthiana plants. One of them, Concord Nursery near Buffalo, New York, sold 20,000 new plants during the winter of 1994 – enough for about 50 acres. A manager there told me: "I've never seen anything like it. We sold commercial quantities of cuttings to people in eleven states." Concord will expand its offerings, and Missouri nurseries planned to have as many as 100,000 new plants available in 1996.

SO FAR, I'VE SOUNDED like a cigar-puffing boomer winding up for a big Everglades land offering. But I should say that not everyone loves Cynthiana's wine. I know one influential eastern viticultural expert who rates it no better than average. And a *Philadelphia Inquirer* wine columnist who had never tasted a Cynthiana wine dismissed Horton's Norton as "uninteresting" and "grapy" in a 1995 story.

Its characteristic flavors are intense and eccentric, not particularly "European," and in most examples not at all polished. But overall the wine is well-liked, and among return customers, it is adored.

Bells and whistles and smoking wheels whirred in my head after my first taste of that 1981 Stone Hill with a girlfriend over sauteed pork tenderloin medallions in prune sauce in a cramped and sticky-humid apartment in Columbia. What I knew was that the Stone Hill was much more flavorful than anything I'd tasted or heard about from anywhere else in eastern America.

Yet, all of these years later now, I don't think Cabernet's noble crown is in danger. Cynthiana is a great grape to grow that can be made into a good wine to drink. It is in the same league as grapes beloved in many European countries for unique regional wines. What keeps it from being a noble grape for noble wine, ironically, is that it is so grapy. Its "flavor profile," as wine gurus would say, can be expanded but the intense grape jam flavor seldom evolves into other flavors with age. In this way, Cynthiana brings to mind the Montepulciano wines of Italy's Abruzzi or the Barbera-Dolcetto blends of Piedmont. Gamza, grown on the Danube plains of Bulgaria, is another native variety prized for its intense grapy flavor. Although connoisseurs wouldn't generally agree, most people in most parts of the world want their good wines, if not their great wines, to taste like grapes. Basic Syrah-based wines of southern France also come to mind, as do potions from the lovely Periquita variety in Portugal; and what about everyday Tuscan Sangiovese? It may not be Concord, but grapy is probably the one best word to describe it.

A well-crafted Cynthiana has a beautiful quixotic color turning to almost blue at its rim. With age, some but not all Cynthiana wines acquire an interesting hint of coffee-toffee in the bouquet, with an ever-present brisk acidity to the flavors that ensures a surprising liveliness even after six or seven years in bottle.

Joe Pollock, the longtime wine columnist for the *St. Louis Post-Dispatch*, regularly reports on tastings of marvelous Stone Hill wines from the '70s and '80s. When joined to delicate characteristics from a *vinifera* grape, Cynthiana also can gain a pretty floral spiciness on a sleek, ultralight frame – bistro-wine par excellence.

It was this potential that made me want to grow it in Pennsylvania.

Almost always, Cynthiana wines in the Midwest are fruity and mouth-filling because they ripen during warm to hot September weather. Red grapes which mature in autumn's first month nearly always translate into generously fruity wines, usually with above-average levels of alcohol and glycerin compounds that add pleasing roundness to the feel of the wine in the mouth. Unfortunately, they also often suffer from high and unstable levels of acidity which can promote unattractive flavors and reduce the life of the wine in bottle. Winemakers in Missouri and Virginia are well-acquainted with such "high PH wines" (PH being a measure of acidity).

Cooler harvest temperatures are better. I reasoned that in western Pennsylvania, with daytime highs in September that are 10 to 15 degrees cooler than in the Midwest, ripening would be extended into the still cooler month of October.

A greater concern was whether there was a warm enough, long enough growing season for Cynthiana to ripen. But there is an old French adage that the best wines result from vines grown successfully at the very edge of the variety's range, and the vinicultural world is full of examples to support the adage (Burgundy's Pinot Noir being perhaps the best example). Cooler ripening weather on a hillside site, I thought, might improve the constitution of Cynthiana's wine by giving it a lighter personality – perhaps even finesse.

Finesse is highly prized, and mountain-grown grapes in many places translate into wines of great felicity; no one knows exactly why, but it's another accepted adage. I hoped to mute the aggressive Cynthiana flavors and smells just enough to then transform the wine through blending with *vinifera*. The result I was after: a medium-bodied wine combining the unique traits of the native American grape with those of more widely encountered, commercially acceptable dry European dinner wines.

The unique characteristics of the Cynthiana grape, when seen in the tradition of distinctive table wines in many other regions of the world, is what makes wine fun, in my mind. All the '90s chatter about great wine-this and great wine-that which emanates from wine retailers and the wine press is useful for jacking up prices. But the closest buddies of Bacchus don't drink wine for the label. No! We seek wines good enough and affordable enough to enjoy routinely with meals – routinely as in daily.

It cannot be said too often that wine can be a healthy part of everyday life. It can lubricate human interaction and unite us with the spirits of the past in a way that other dinner guests cannot. It's as fundamental an accoutrement as spring water from a dewy pitcher, crisp greens, chewy bread, and flowing conversation.

I embrace "great wine" with the proper esteem, and don't throw the term around recklessly. My toleration for pomposity is low, and I avoid association when I can with people who use wine as a weapon in class warfare. I am suspicious of self-important, coded talk about wine. I despise numerical ratings. Plus, I have a twisted sense of parsimony: I will always take a case of merely above average wine, reasonably honest and pure, over a bottle or two of greatness.

Truthfully, I don't presume to be worth great wine very often, and I don't believe the glossy wine sheets that insist majesty can be bought 'round the corner for $12 and drunk tonight.

Remembering my formative years as a wine-lover, I can say that when I tasted that '81 Stone Hill I immediately thought it was good but that it could be better. Its sheer intensity was both a liability and a great starting point, it seemed.

From that day forward, I wanted to make wine from Cynthiana that expressed my ideas about beauty, generosity, and the sublime.

Today I can add to this formula, perhaps above all other pursuits, a desire for my Cynthiana wine to express my thinking as a farmer more so than as a winemaker.

-three-

Autumn 1992

ESSENTIAL PREPARATIONS for Year 2 in the vineyard revolved around the trellis. A grid of parallel steel wires had to be strung between the posts, and the early morning of the first Friday in November 1992 was a bone-chiller on the hillside at Scenery Hill. My father-in-law, his brother-in-law, and a couple of my friends gathered to help. At 7 a.m. we were all there, in a frosty-breathed circle.

The trees were ablaze, and when the leaves are on, only hayfields interrupt the wall of solid woods that the hillside faces mainly to the south and West, to the horizon where West Virginia is.

The site looked especially postcard-beautiful that morning. And I know the dramatic vista contributed greatly to my early romanticism about all things farming. To paraphrase author Edward Abbey, romanticism isn't worth much except for inspiration. Why shouldn't I be thrilled to be part of this landscape? Yosemite Valley's picturesque appeal is what inspired John Muir's earliest work on its behalf. Only later did his real knowledge and accomplishments come.

At Scenery Hill, with this expanse a glance away for eight to twelve hours a day, I concentrated. The thinking under my hat in the hours before fatigue tormented comprehension criss-crossed new terrain. After my second or third session at Scenery Hill, I had stopped taking along a watch. On high perch in this heroic place, the rhythms of exertion, rest, and awe propelled me through time.

A subtle change had presented itself during that first season. I know it now better, by recollection, and understand more of its meaning. Whenever I thought about the vineyard, the vantage point that came most readily to me, that recurred quickest, had shifted. When I started, I recall that I would remember the place from the vineyard site: me looking out; but gradually the recurrent view became one that included me within the landscape, as if I were looking at me hoeing, me shoveling, me clipping – me seen working from, say, the next hill over.

As I became more and more devoted to the plants and to their husbandry, I grew also to especially love to see visitors' reactions to the view.

On that cold morning in November 1992, all the wire-stringers stamped around sipping coffee. As the hillside grew brighter, we turned more and more toward the sun, as insects warming their wings. As we looked south, our talk fell on just the beauty of the hill. "You almost don't even notice the cold," somebody said.

Then, as rarely happens with a group of people nowadays, the men did not fight the silence when it came.

Everyone looked at each other, smiling and shivering. No one grew self-conscious. The silence held for a minute or maybe a little more.

A steely wind warned of winter, but a cloudless sky of southerly sun single-handedly would save the morning. "Ready for a little work, guys?"

Within minutes, worry arose when it was revealed that I really didn't know what I was doing. Stretching wire for the trellis was something that I'd only read about. Some of the fellows, the younger ones, remarked that this was a familiar refrain. "Well, we'll have to figure it out as we go," I said sheepishly.

The learning curve was steep and spiky. The first length of wire we stretched, 210 feet, snapped when we cut it and whipped half-way back down the row. Men dove headlong before its wicked curl.

"That stuff'll cut your head off," huffed my father-in-law John, getting back on his feet, his pants smeared with mud. I did not think there would be danger involved, and was thankful no one was hurt.

Gradually the cuts were contained, and we found the rhythm for stretching the wire, stringing it on steel brads pounded into the posts, and tying it off at the ends. The skeleton of a vineyard began to take shape.

The gents put in a full shift, in sun till lunch, in a bitter cold shadow by the end. Double shots of Amaretto di Saranno was the pay for the day, with promises of wine when the grapes came in.

I worked to get all the wire cut while I had help, because I knew I'd have to come back and string long stretches alone.

CYNTHIANA IN AMERICA. Where to pick up its quirky journey?

Many people probably don't realize how beloved grape varieties are. I know an Italian immigrant winegrower who brought twigs of his favorite variety in the form of crosses in his luggage, and convinced immigration officials they were religious objects. The *vitis* is a botanical order legendary for arousing intense loyalties. Its story is full of wayfarers and wanderers, luxury and decadence, secret genealogies and whispered myths.

Many wine grapes have fantabulous "creation stories," and Cynthiana claims a shadowy origin to match any. Throughout its history, this orphan with the twinkle in its glass created a stir wherever it took root. That mysterious air – its impossibly deep, nearly black robe; its velvety texture; its penetrating aroma and flavor – definitely helps in marketing the wine. But, as we all know, a questionable past also has its disadvantages.

Cynthiana's relatively long history as a cultivated variety, back to the early nineteenth century, is a mixed blessing. While recorded commentary of all manner exists, much is of a dubious nature. Norton was described in texts and catalogs for a century and a half as distinct from Cynthiana and many growers insist there are subtle distinctions in the field. Genetically, though, these two examples of the species *vitis aestivalis* are the same.

"Isozyme analysis have, to date, revealed no differences," says Charles Edson, citing the most sophisticated genetic tests available. Edson, an extension specialist now at Michigan State University, was part of the research team that studied the grape for Missouri's industry in the early 1990s at the State Fruit Experiment Station of Southwest Missouri State University.

Many authorities previously concluded that equipment and laboratory procedures were not sophisticated enough to isolate the differences between the two vines. Isozyme testing, which incorporates cutting-edge computer technology, was a major leap forward, and the conclusion that Cynthiana and Norton were identical surprised many people.

In fact, "surprised" is a mild word. Many growers dismissed the findings because they felt certain they had seen differences in the vineyard.

The scientists, however, persisted. Using similar equipment and procedures, researchers in 1992 at Cornell University in New York reached the same conclusion as their counterparts had in Missouri.

To this day plenty of growers and winemakers do not accept the findings. As a result, most midwestern wineries market Cynthiana wines as a lighter drink for immediate enjoyment, while the wine from Norton, generally, is presented as the one for longer aging. Often, the distinctions are not justified, but the cash registers suggest that consumers don't care.

As wine history, the story is a fascinating footnote to America's tortured relationship with wine. The very first newcomers to the continent tried to use native grapes to make wine, with little success. Today, the wine industry is weighed down tremendously by federal, state, and local regulators who lump together purveyors of rot-gut grain alcohol and those fermenting grapes to facilitate the collection of excise taxes and expensive permits. (For a small winery, annual governmental fees and permits amount to a minimum of 20 cents a bottle, and then there's excise tax to be paid by the gallon and then sales tax.)

Most of the taxes and regulations were born in the days of trading with Native Americans on the western frontier, and later, in trying to bust up Al Capone and his boys. Regulators act like they suspect small wineries deal in contraband on the side. In France, an artisan winegrower can make and sell wine in his garage, with little legal interference. In America, one can send radioactive waste by mail, yet many states forbid wine to be shipped by mail – in the age of the Internet!

Given the distractions for those trying to make a living with wine, it's not surprising that to this day there is still no agreement on the exact identity of the one exceptional native grape – Cynthiana – for making dry red table wines in America. And astonishingly, it was under our noses all along.

Much has been written about the matter in plant science and wine industry journals, as graduate students and their professors continue to explore the variety's past. Probably because of the grape's commercial importance in the Midwest, university research continues to be funded. One recent and exciting find, also from Missouri's experiment station, is that Cynthiana possesses up to twice the amount of the chemical agent in red wine grapes (reservatrol) which widely publicized medical research links to the health benefits from drinking moderate quantities of red wine.

As for the tantalizing history of Cynthiana, though, no account in recent years surpasses a summary of the controversy published nearly a century ago.

The author was U.P. Hedrick. He would go on to direct Cornell's esteemed school of horticulture and to become, arguably, the leading figure in American horticulture between 1920 and 1940. As a researcher at Cornell in the first decade of the century, Hedrick was part of a team that mounted several impressive studies of the nation's fruit farming. The studies were then published by the New York legislature, whose members used the handsome books mainly as freebie handouts to growers – back in the days when the "farm vote" mattered.

Hedrick's account of the Cynthiana/Norton controversy appeared in his *Grapes of New York* (1908), a scholarly classic which rare book dealers especially prize for its fine color paintings of several dozen grapes. More than 1,000 varieties are cited.

"The botanical differences of the two varieties," Hedrick writes, "are not greater than might be attributed to environment, soil, climate and culture; but side by side the two grapes ripen at different times, and the quality of the fruit, and more particularly of the wine, is such that the varieties must be considered distinct.

"The distinction," he adds wryly, "should be maintained, for Cynthiana is the better grape of the two."

Although equipment and methods for plant research only faintly resemble those in Hedrick's day, great innovations often cannot alter conclusions when nature is the object under scrutiny: although the modern verdict on the similarities between Norton and Cynthiana must stand, many people in the industry will never accept it.

In his 1993 article about Missouri wines, *Gourmet* wine columnist Gerald Asher touched on the debate. He doesn't refer to Hedrick's 1908 book, but he does remark on the mind-bending complexity of Cornell's 1992 research. "Either the two always were one," as the Cornell/Missouri research shows, writes Asher, "or, if different, then all present plantings, under whichever name . . . must have been propagated from just one version of the two."

Well, okay. Enough. We can't go on like this. We must go back. A complete telling of the story must begin almost a century before Hedrick's writing.

THE YEAR IS 1825. Many in the young nation are engaged in a race to create, name, and market new varieties of shrubbery, trees, and other plants that Americans might consider useful and attractive. An interest in native plants was a national obsession during the first three decades of the nineteenth century, and hardly ebbed until the Civil War. The competition was intense, patriotic, and macho – or at least awfully masculine. Occasionally, very occasionally, it was even lucrative.

One of those hell-bent on making his mark was Dr. D.N. Norton of Richmond, Virginia. The good doctor experimented with a number of species, but the grape attributed to Dr. Norton, who brought no other plants to commercial prominence, was so accidental that no one has determined the varieties he crossed to produce his namesake hybrid.

John McGrew has come closer than anyone. The retired U.S. Department of Agriculture extension specialist's research about the doctor and his Norton grape occupied the better part of two years in the late 1980s. Exactness is not possible, McGrew concluded. "A real problem is that there's no known description of Dr. Norton's grounds," he told me when we met at a conference in 1990. I'd heard that McGrew had spent some time snooping around Richmond's archival collections. "But I can't find anything about his garden in any historical papers," he said. "All that is known comes from second-hand accounts – statements about him and his work in the writings of others."

Still, McGrew figures he has a pretty good idea of how Dr. Norton made his discovery. He reasons that since grapes from seeds often mature into plants with characteristics somewhat different from their parents', the original Norton vine grew from the seed of a grape genetically related.

Certainly *aestivalis* grows in the Richmond area. McGrew guesses the winning "seedling" was one of many others the doctor planted in his garden. Because grapes mutate so readily from seeds, planting the pips is the easiest way to "create" new varieties. Creating new varieties from seed is certainly much easier, requires less technical skill, than gathering pollen and manipulating it among the tiny flowers on growing vines. Who knows – maybe the seedling caught the doctor's attention as he ambled past his compost pile one day; or perhaps a robin robbed a grape from Norton's garden, digested it, and planted the seed for him with a drop of fertilizer to boot. It happens.

Even though Norton was a physician, professional training in horticultural experimentation was scarce. As was true of most men pursuing their interest in plants in 1820, he most likely was a backyard tinkerer – a hobby hybridist.

Based on when the grape is known to have been first offered for sale at a commercial nursery (1830), McGrew figures Dr. Norton isolated the seedling as early as 1817, and perhaps as late as 1823 or '24. Dr. Norton would have spent most of the decade of the 1820s propagating the vine – with difficulty. For reasons still unknown, the species will not produce roots routinely from "cuttings" (branches clipped off the plant and buried in soil to force roots to grow from the clipping). Most varieties root fairly easily using this technique. "But *aestivalis* is just one of those species that doesn't," notes McGrew. "That's been one of the factors that has held it back as a commercial variety."

What horticulturists do with hard-to-root plants is likely what Dr. Norton did. He probably covered a cane from a growing vine in shallow soil to force roots to grow from the covered buds and nodes. This trick, called "layering" in the nursery trade, is one of the grape plant's own survival traits. Its ready-to-root personality makes *vitis* a highly successful competitor in the world's temperate and semi-temperate latitudes.

This can be confirmed by an average walk in the woods. Trying to find the original trunk of a single wild grape plant is nearly impossible because everywhere the vine runs along the forest floor it sends out new roots from nodes covered by moist humus.

New leafy growth – a potential new plant – shoots up above ground. In this way, the plant can withstand great vagaries; if all of its roots could be dug up at once, or, say, frozen during a bitter winter, the vine would die. It will regenerate, though, from any undamaged node in contact with damp soil by sending out roots from the covered bud.

Wild grapes can be a scourge in many forests and woodlots. After decades of growth, their immense weight is enough to bend and uproot large trees. In my city, for example, park officials have voiced much concern about damage to trees in two beloved parks. The killing of trees is not uncommon; uprooting occurs with surprising frequency during heavy snows. I found trees felled in this way in the Allegheny Mountains during the harsh, snowy winter of 1993-94. The snowpack built up on the dense maze of canes clinging to the tree, increasing by many times the weight on the host. In one spot, I counted thirteen valuable hardwoods downed, all of them forty to fifty years old – their prime age for board lumber.

The summer before, I also had noticed how little sunlight reached the forest floor around those same trees because of the canopy of wild vines. Wild grapes spread quickly in exposed sunny areas of the forest, then race to shade out competitors with their giant floppy leaves.

Once a potential new plant shoots up from a covered cane, the cane can be clipped on both sides of the new growth. Roots below, leaves above – presto, a new plant. And unlike propagation from seeds, these new plants are identical to the original. Layering is tedious and time-consuming but a sure-fire way to raise plants that won't root from cuttings. (I've done it with Cynthiana myself.)

Dr. Norton probably stuck with the method, turning out enough young plants to offer a bunch for sale after several years. This make sense. As McGrew reasons, Dr. Norton would have learned first-hand after three or four growing seasons that his Norton's Virginia Seedling was a handsome picture of vigor and health. Undoubtedly, it was as free from the grape's typical pests as any variety he had grown. (There are very, very few varieties known anywhere in the world that resist disease as well or grow as vigorously.)

Maybe, just maybe, the Norton's joyful growth is why the doctor chose to name it for himself, instead of honoring a favorite daughter, pony, stud ram, or horticultural comrade, as was the custom of the day. (Angeline, Iona, Lenoir, Noah, and Stark's Star are some of the more straightforward examples.)

Some reports, more reliable than most from the era, contend that Dr. Norton's homemade claret – not the grape itself – was what the public clamored for most around his native Richmond. But however it was that the news traveled, the Norton variety reached William Robert Prince by 1830.

This fact is known, among precious few in the saga, because that is the year of publication for Prince's two-volume *A Treatise on the Vine, Pomological Manual.* Prince unceremoniously describes Norton among hundreds of other grape plants in his commercial nursery. His work is considered the first of real consequence on viticulture to be published in America.

Some background on Prince is in order, and again, I cannot do better than Hedrick:

William Robert Prince, fourth proprietor of the Prince
Nursery and Linnaean Botanic Garden, Flushing, New York,
was born in 1795 and died in 1869. Prince was without
question the most capable horticulturist of his time and an
economic botanist of note. His love of horticulture and
botany was a heritage from at least three paternal ancestors,
all noted in these branches of science, and all of whom he
apparently surpassed in mental capacity, intellectual training
and energy.

As if to emphasize the shortcomings of Prince's peers, Hedrick notes that
the nurseryman's writings were "characterized by a clear, vigorous style and
by accuracy in statement." Hedrick became a famous American horticulturist – a London newspaper, reviewing his history of horticulture in the 1940s,
called his grasp of the subject "staggering" – and in his commendations of
Prince, and in possessing a similar literary forcefulness, Hedrick hints at feeling a strong kinship.

Hedrick continues the story masterfully in his description of Norton in
Grapes of New York; he notes that Dr. Norton had informed Prince that his
namesake originated from the seed of two other varieties. The doctor told
Prince the varieties were Bland and Miller's Burgundy, which were growing
near one another in his garden. But, continues Hedrick:

This parentage, it appeared later, was undoubtedly an error
as the Norton shows none of the characters of either Bland
or Miller's Burgundy. Prince's description leaves little doubt
that his Norton was the Norton of to-day. In 1861 there was
an article published in the *Horticulturist* by a Mr. Lemosy
saying that the original Norton had been discovered in 1835
by his father, Dr. F.A. Lemosy of Richmond, Virginia, on an
island in the James River and that Dr. Norton secured the
variety from this source.

The Lemosy angle would come to haunt Dr. Norton. For many decades
after the journal article cited by Hedrick, the man (Dr. Norton) who had
been credited in the three previous decades with the gift of this fabulous little
grape to America – a grape that, by 1850, was delighting growers and international wine connoisseurs alike – was suspected of presenting as his own

what he had found growing wild on a riverbank.

It seems the man who had created the hybrid and named the grape was unofficially but effectively stripped of honors.

ON THREE OF THE FOUR DAYS it took for me to string the wires for the trellis at Scenery Hill, I worked alone from early in the morning till dark. I packed my food in, camped on the hill, and didn't see a soul for three days.

Thoughts ranged from earliest childhood to college and marriage, then from second marriage back to childhood. I realized later it was the most number of waking hours I'd spent entirely alone in . . . in perhaps my whole life.

Winter grew closer with each passing hour, with less and less sun and more and more wind. Trudging up and down the rows, my wind-burned face felt like it had been lightly sand-papered. Blood pumping for probably 35 hours, my core was a volcano.

On the last day, a landscape artist friend from Pittsburgh came and painted the fading ochres and purples of the late year. The 1992 growing season, an excellent one for starting a vineyard with rains throughout the summer that kept the young plants growing, ended with all leaves blown from the trees in a big wind that rose after lunch and delivered flying snowflakes.

Where blazing orange and red cloaks ruled the week before, bare branches reigned. It was the second week of November and the promises of a new season were safely stowed away on each vine. Cynthiana's plump buds were puppy nipples.

AS THE LEMOSY THEORY made its rounds, a group of German immigrants living in Philadelphia but itchy to move on bought several hundred acres beside the Missouri River in Gasconade County, Missouri. They proceeded to build a town, Hermann, with a main street exactly 1 foot wider than Philadelphia's Market Street.

By the time their little nirvana might be considered a place with staying power (the early 1850s), these Germans had established a local economy as tied to wine as any ever in the New World. And one grape above all the others had solidified its influence in the hills around Hermann (as well as in Arkansas and Virginia at roughly the same time). Missouri essayist, politician, and winegrower Friedrich Muench proclaimed the little blue grape a gift "worth millions" to his new home, for the red wine of Cynthiana, he boasted, "when three or four years old, is hardly to be surpassed."

The appearance of the article about the Lemosy theory in a respected journal, the *Horticulturist*, gave the theory clout. Commentators and nursery catalogs were quick to quote it. Circulars in the 1870s from nurseries that sold the grape, such as Bush & Son & Meissner near St. Louis, credited Dr. Norton, but by 1883 the catalogs from the renowned firm gave one "Dr. Lemosq" the honors. Bush & Son's publications included a fruit-growing manual, and were so popular that they became college agricultural texts. The firm was among the Missouri nurseries credited with saving Europe's vineyards in the late 19th century after the phylloxera crisis. Their fruit-growing guides were even translated into French and Italian.

In its 1883 catalog, Bush & Son, noting that Dr. Norton had propagated the vine by "transplanting layers from the original vine to his garden," put a bizarre twist on the known truth by adding that Dr. Norton had "introduced it to public notice." Perhaps the company was unwilling to breathe the name of its competitor, Prince. Whatever the cause, the curious words chosen by the influential midwestern nursery to describe Cynthiana's provenance were to be repeated dozens of times in print thereafter.

The one-page account in 1906 of the grape's discovery by Liberty Hyde Bailey, the well-regarded dean of horticulture at Cornell who described Norton in his popular book as an epoch-maker, is virtually identical to the falsity spread by Bush & Son.

The confusion should have persisted for only two more years – a total of almost 50 – because in 1908 Hedrick came along in *Grapes of New York* to restore sanity. He does not mince words: "Since Dr. Norton had sent this variety to Prince prior to 1830, the [Lemosy] story is evidently wrong as to dates and is suspicious as to facts."

"It is probable," he concludes, "that the true history of Norton will never be known."

Thomas Munson, a pioneering hybridist in turn-of-the-century Texas whose drawings of grapes are considered a national treasure in the U.S. agriculture library in suburban Washington, undoubtedly had read Hedrick's description. Yet Munson also denied Dr. Norton his due when his eminently scholarly *Foundations of American Grape Culture* appeared in 1911. Munson repeats the Lemosy theory, glossing over Hedrick's point that Lemosy could not have "discovered" the variety in 1835 if Dr. Norton had sent it to Prince five years before that.

As myth is known for staying power, Gerald Asher in his 1993 *Gourmet* piece calls the Lemosy theory the "accepted origin."

Midwestern wineries love all the intrigue. For new customers coming through the door, the name controversy heightens the allure of Cynthiana's wine. Most sellers happily supply a short recitation. And if you own a small winery five or ten miles from a major two-lane highway, anything that makes people seek out your wine is a godsend. At least with Cynthiana, they'll probably be coming back.

I consider my vines Cynthiana, but tend to use the name interchangeably with Norton. If one works with the varieties, a choice is required or otherwise a lot of time is chewed up saying "Norton, er . . . Cynthiana" when talking with growers, winemakers, writers, retailers, wholesalers, restaurateurs, tasting panelists, the press, the public. Wives.

In 1992, searching for sources of rooted cuttings of Cynthiana, I found a nursery near Buffalo that had them. The firm's catalog called the variety Norton, even though I knew the Arkansas nurseryman who had supplied the Buffalo firm with cuttings for propagation insists his vines are Cynthiana. When my plants arrived from the nursery, a cryptic summary of the whole sweeping mess was printed on a tiny piece of clammy paper stuffed in among the damp packing matter covering the roots.

Down on my knees in the field to start planting them, I opened the shipping container and turned to rubber laughing at the little missive inside: "Norton. (Syn. Cynthiana). Found wild on Cedar Island in the James River...." Discoverer: "F.A. Lemosque. Named and introduced by Dr. R.N. Norton."

-four-

ABOUT HALF-PAST MIDNIGHT one snowy early morning in mid-January 1993, right after that first season of growing grapes, I was transferring the last container of wine in my makeshift basement *weinstub* into another vessel ("racking" the wine, as the act is termed) when a partial-thought struck: "Pinot Noir."

Squirreled away was a 5-gallon carboy of Pinot wine that I had made from Lake Erie-area grapes. I pulled it out, and began making mixes with the Cynthiana wine I had made that fall from Virginia-grown grapes. Playing around with various ratios, I found that 15 percent Pinot tamed the Cynthiana while propping up the flavors in the mid-range, toning down the aggressively grapy smell, and adding a hard-to-explain but distinctly *vinifera* element.

I commented in my notes: "real elegance; velvety, taut, and restrained – all qualities I didn't think could be achieved with the sort of blunt, direct soul of Cynthiana."

The rest seemed fairly evident. I added a little Chambourcin wine I'd made from the French hybrid grape now very popular in the eastern U.S., to get a little more complexity in the fruit aromas and flavors. I also put in some Vidal Blanc because a white wine sort of stretches out the more dominant flavors from the reds. (I believe it was Baron Ricasoli, credited with the modern recipe for Tuscany's Chianti Classico, who said that a little splash of the white Malvasia was essential in his region's blended reds, because for some reason it brought all the other flavors into sharper focus.) Satisfied roughly with the trial blend, I compiled a more exact one, adding Pinot,

Chambourcin, and Vidal to the Cynthiana base in 1 percent increments until I reached the point I liked best; then I went beyond that point, and backed up again, just to check myself.

By then, it was 2 a.m., and the hours of sane judgment were long since past while a wife, long ago having given up on me, was tucked away fast asleep.

The next night, as I was climbing the stairs to watch television, I stopped on the landing and in ten seconds invalidated the bleary-eyed hours of blending by pouring two wines with ratios of Cynthiana 10 percent apart. There on the landing, I smelled, sipped, and swirled each sample around in my mouth: ah, half-way in between was just right.

The wine had balance. It had a wonderful berry, spicy, minty aroma. It had a stirring dash of what tasted like wild grape juice. It was direct, lush, and generous.

Paired two nights later with a black bean casserole, lightly cayenned, the spicy aroma and ribbon candy fruitiness played just right. (Think about it, a good bean wine is hard to find.) The experience is one reason I no longer take part in "blind tasting" tournaments or otherwise rule on wines without dinner food in the other hand: many great wines don't need food, while less showy but more sublime wines need food to draw out their charms.

The dinner segment of the competition now complete, I could reflect on having concocted a basic but distinctive regional wine, expressing a unique combination of climate, soil, and characteristics from three very different types of grapes from eastern America.

Only in eastern America, among all other regions in the world, are so many different species of grapes grown for wine-making. The possibilities for blending are immense (and symbolic, as well, of the region's "melting pot" history), yet few vintners take advantage of the possibilities. Eastern America's winemakers seem content by and large to dabble with the same *vinifera* wines made in Europe and California, and to rely on inferior wines from French hybrid grapes for the bulk of production.

A lot of eastern winemakers will bristle at this statement. In defense, I shall note that the French, who developed hybrid grapes for growing in non-traditional wine districts, all but abandoned hybrid grapes during the last two decades. Chambourcin, in fact, is really the only one that stuck. It is used fairly widely in the Loire Valley of France for *vin du pays*. After nearly a half-century of experimentation in France, hybrids were found to offer no appreciable advantages over *vinifera* grapes in the vineyard or in the cellar.

In America, however, while the planting of hybrids has slowed dramatically in the 1990s, at the expense of *vinifera*, the eastern wine industry is still based on their culture.

As for the blended wine I made that winter night from Cynthiana, all I can say is that I liked it best, as did every person who tasted it during the following weeks and months. It fulfilled my objective of making a wine that didn't taste like any other. That was what mattered then: my wine, wine unique to my ego, was the objective.

THE UNINITIATED ARE SURELY TEMPTED to conclude after hearing the peculiar histrionics of the Cynthiana/Norton dispute that it doesn't really matter. What's in a name, right? But in Arkansas and Missouri, states where the majority of wine from the grape is being made, the Cynthiana/ Norton dispute does figure in: a varietal name may end up on a label, and an attractive name is often enough to win new customers.

Robert Scheef probably knows as much as anyone about the region's vinicultural history. His *Vintage Missouri* (1991) was the first modern book on the Missouri industry. (Scheef's book also discusses the Arkansas wine industry, which is much smaller than Missouri's.) The thirty-something Scheef is a free-lance writer who makes his home in a comfortable St. Louis suburb. His research for the book carried him through nearly four years, after he had returned to his home state after living for several years in California.

During the course of his research, Scheef said when we talked in 1995, he became especially interested in the identity debate about Cynthiana and Norton. He condenses the debate this way: "If there is a difference in the grapes, then it's so minor, so miniscule – it's at the level of micro-botany.

"What difference does it make? Well, in Hermann, it matters because they're claiming their vines pre-date the Civil War. And they're claiming they're Norton." The grape and its wine are referred to almost exclusively as Norton in this, the original and ethnically Germanic core of the state's wineland.

Modern Hermannites hold their breath every time a new study comes out, Scheef jokes, because it could be a little embarrassing – no catastrophe, but embarrassing – if the grapes planted in the 1850s that Stone Hill Winery includes in its famous Norton wine were judged, instead, to be Cynthiana. "And I think Cynthiana is a more melodic, more flattering name than Norton," says Scheef. "Norton's not a pretty name, not at all."

I agreed. "But still," I said, "you can't argue with what Stone Hill has done." Stone Hill put the wine on the map and the firm still sells the most of it. And they've done it using the Norton name. "Apparently, customers don't care as much about the name as everyone fears they do," I told Scheef.

Stone Hill's owner James Held and winemaker David Johnson have commented extensively about the company's vines in the newspapers and state trade association circulars. Theirs was once the country's third largest winery, and numerous independent sources place vines known as Norton at Stone Hill's historic property two decades before a vine that locals called Cynthiana was first mentioned in the thriving midwestern horticulture press of the 1870s.

Johnson told me in a 1986 interview that the "small number" of old vines at Stone Hill – "oh, a couple of acres' worth" – always produced the richest, best wine. "Those wines have absolute world-class appeal. We make them here the way great Bordeaux is made," fully-extracted, dense in color, and tannic from "about two years in oak barrels."

Some of the winery's early '80s Nortons are said to be aging well still. By the middle part of that decade, Stone Hill was engaged in an ambitious planting program to approximately quadruple its production of the wine.

Stone Hill's winemaker had no reason to pump up the debate about the grape's name. He was unequivocal: "We sell all we can make and the name wouldn't matter."

Perhaps the debate most of all confirms just how young Cynthiana is by global standards as a vine, and as a wine of importance. The competition matters less for those wineries with established customers than for newcomers looking for a niche. Pinot Noir, another variety known for its clonal variations, must have gone through similar exorcisms when its value to Burgundy was realized by farmers there a thousand years ago. Proprietor-growers, also vinters usually, surely noticed subtle differences between their Pinot vines and wines and those from a neighbor's hill on the other side of the stone wall. Today, growers in Burgundy make quite a fuss over clones, though the discussions are too arcane to rate regular coverage in the popular wine press.

So it is with Cynthiana. At once exhilarating and distressing to consider, the grape is in the early, painful stages of earning a reputation. Whether it takes ten more years or a hundred to be as well-known as Cabernet – even among wine-drinkers, much less the general public – is impossible to predict. After all, there were earlier enthusiasms but Cynthiana's reputation from the last century did not endure.

Discussing all the possibilities by phone – me sipping a glass of the very item, my own homemade, as we talked – Scheef and I agreed that Dr. Norton's creation story, which has the Norton resulting from a chance crossing of a *vitis vinifera* and a native American species (*vitis labrusca*, such as Concord), could be wrong – or it could be really wrong. Maybe the doctor did produce his namesake by crossing *vinifera* with *labrusca*, but probably, as U.P. Hedrick contended, they were not the two grapes Dr. Norton named. Or . . . maybe Lemosy was also partly correct: maybe Dr. Norton did obtain the vine from the wild before propagating it and sending it to Prince in 1830, and this became clear to Lemosy when he came forward five years later with an identical-looking grape that he had found along the James River.

Scheef reasoned, "It's good if the wine writers talk about it –"

– "though," I finished, "it's still mostly state wine writers and not the *Wine Spectator*."

Then he said, "How about this? Everyone seems to agree that Cynthiana came from Arkansas. Say it's a wild vine. Both Cynthiana and Norton are *vitis aestivalis. Aestivalis* grows wild in Virginia, too."

"Yeah, yeah, they know that both grapes are *aestivalis*," I said. "It grows wild all over the southeastern part of the country. A northern variant, a subspecies – which shows the species' tendency to mutate – grows up here in Pennsylvania."

"What you have," Scheef said, "is clones of the same variety. It's really not that unusual, you know. Lots of grapes have clones."

Then we rattled on for another fifteen minutes about Burgundy and Pinot Noir clones, about Pinot Droit and Pinot Meunier and Pinot St. George and Gamay Beaujolais, which is actually a true Pinot Noir – a clone of Pinot Noir. Gamay Noir, not G. Beaujolais, is the true Gamay of France's Beaujolais. And that's the truth.

Anyway, several factors are more important to the outcome of the finished wine than whatever shade of difference might exist between clones. For instance, in the vineyard, trellis systems can have a more profound effect, with systems that spread the foliage over a large area and allow more sunlight into the canopy producing riper grapes. In the cellar, the amount of time the grapes soak ("macerate") in contact with their skins greatly affects the wine's personality. Even though several central Missouri producers in recent years have started to market wines as Cynthiana that are more supple and earlier maturing, there is no unanimity in Missouri, much less among growers and producers in all the other states where the grape thrives.

Tom Post of Post Winery in Altus, Arkansas, was very firm about what he wished the grape plants to be called that he sold to me in 1992. (Between Post and Concord Nursery in Buffalo, I was able to secure all I needed.) Post didn't mind speaking about the north-south rift, either: "Now, up in Missouri, they grow the Norton, I guess. But ours are Cynthiana."

"The two states don't get along, do they?" I asked, not having told him yet that I had grown up in southeast Missouri. He thought he was just dealing with someone from "out East."

"Well, sir," he said, in the courtly tone that he still uses with me even though he knows where I'm from now and we talk frequently by phone, "not on some things, no they don't."

I asked if he knew the origin of the story that Cynthiana was found growing wild in Arkansas. He allowed that he did not but that every grower "in *Arkansas* as far back as you want to go" (his emphasis) has repeated the truism to him. I am in no position to argue, because I have benefitted from Tom Post's wisdom and experience on several occasions. (Just as he said, the potassium and phosphorus in a handful of turkey manure, thrown into each hole at planting, made the plants grow so vigorously that they were to produce fruit in only their second year – a year ahead of the standard schedule.) But when I've tried to talk about the fact that even if the two varieties are not the same, their wines are so close (I think those were almost my exact words), he has said every time, "Well, all I know is it's Cynthiana that we grow."

FOR EIGHT YEARS or so before my midnight breakthrough in 1993, I had experimented as a home winemaker with blends of wine from Cynthiana and various grapes. Like Tom Post, I had a conviction based on others' experiences. As I've said, my conviction was that adding other flavors, textures, and smells would make a better wine than straight Cynthiana. I believed it because so much of the world's most enduring and traditional red wines are in fact blended wines.

Also true about wine is that it's one of those enterprises in which the homemade can be as good as the professional. This is especially the case with dry red table wines, mainly because the process is so simple.

As Nicholas Faith points out in his wonderful 1975 history of Bordeaux, peasant grower-producers have always dominated the wine trade along the Gironde (except, arguably, in the two decades since his book). "Great claret," Faith notes, "requires only the skills – though elevated to the highest level – normally associated with agricultural production." Quality grapes are certainly needed, but the human "qualities required are those of the skilled husbandman, not of the industrialist."

To become proficient in winemaking, one can read, form a fair idea of what he likes by drinking wines regularly, and then age his finished efforts properly. Amazingly good results may rise from home cellars. I learned this the first year I made a hundred gallons in my basement. One of my first wines, a 1991 white from a common French hybrid grape, Vidal Blanc, was the runaway favorite in an eastern Pennsylvania tasting of gold and silver medal Vidal wines from commercial wineries in nine states.

It was my first attempt at white wine, but I'd been reading about how to do it for ten years. I remembered the tasty wines I'd had from the same grape and I knew the other varieties related to Vidal and the sorts of wines made from them in other regions. With those two critical bits of knowledge, it was not difficult to deduce the method for making the sort of wine I wanted mine to be.

From the moment my wine wiped out all those medal-winners, I knew I would never be satisfied – at home or as a professional – with making look-alikes of Europe's or California's good wines. I would never be content to say in ten years, as so many winemakers are, that my "award-winning wines are among the finest in the state."

I wanted whole new flavors, my standards were the finest wines in the world, and I refused to merely imitate anyone.

The husbandman has a craft mentality. He is an artisan. He learns from one task to the next, bearing the long dull hours and waiting for experience, thoughtfully applied, to become expertise.

Learning through an apprenticeship of one's own making is bound to create memories both good and horrifying. The first year that Nadine and I picked grapes in Virginia, for instance, we worked in the sun all day and drove home all night. Not knowing that we should seal the containers holding the grapes led to a seven-hour flight of terror with dime-sized, clear-colored spiders having the run of the hatchback and us.

These days we keep the picked grapes outside all the way to the crusher.

The following September, the next vintage, found us in York County, Pennsylvania, stalking Cabernet Sauvignon. I'd planned to pick 1,100 pounds. Four inches of rain, the worst in two months, fell as we drove across the Pennsylvania mountains. When grapes are almost ripe and that much rain comes, they can swell and crack; along the crack, where the juicy flesh is exposed to air, mold grows, making little downy fissures. It doesn't take much mold to foul the wine. The next morning, a breezy Sunday, was enchanted, "airish" you'd call it, but with the smell of winter, not playfulness, in the wind. Though the breeze dried up the remaining water drops on the clusters, the damage was done. We were able to pick only 200 pounds, and I believe we got most every grape that wasn't moldy. It was real ugly. I felt so sorry for the owner.

I've picked grapes below thickening skies, thunder, and angry clouds all day, and on afternoons so sunny and hot that my last dribble of energy could barely lift the last bucket of the day.

I've trod Cynthiana with bare feet at dusk in truck-bed fermentors at 3,000 feet in Maryland's mountains as a buddy spread a dinner of road-bought barbeque on a state park picnic table. There's been a lot of night driving, and fortunately very little was done alone.

On a couple of occasions, I bought newly fermented Cynthiana and French hybrid reds in central Missouri, and also worked that one season with Larry Carver at his winery. Then I did my harvest stint in 1986 in California, and so I got to learn a lot about Cabernet Sauvignon, Cabernet

Franc, and Zinfandel. In between and since, I fooled around with many blends from commercial wines.

I have tasted dozens of samples of Cynthiana wines on travels in Missouri and Arkansas, and served as a judge at commercial wine competitions at the Missouri State Fair and Indiana State Fair. One year at the Missouri Fair, I tasted 120 wines and was able to pick out six of the seven Cynthiana wines. I studied and read about wine continually, socialized with wine-appreciators, and went to quite a few wine tastings. I visited perhaps 150 wineries in twenty or so states.

I searched out Sicilian, Grecian, and Corsican red wines that were not easy to find for sale in America. In a Slavic neighborhood in Chicago, I once encountered the gloriously rustic peasant reds from Slovenia's native grapes, and another time I carted home from New York fourteen bottles of inexpensive Spanish wines from blends mainly of Grenache, Carignan, and Tempranillo.

By the early 1990s, my tastings of different red wines, from just about every U.S. state or country that made them, had cleared 1,000. That's a fair but conservative estimate. The point is I had formed a fair opinion of how a distinctive wine from Cynthiana might taste.

MY HUNCH ALL ALONG was that reasonably astute wine judges, like the general public they represent, could not discern a pattern among wines named "Cynthiana" and those named "Norton." In addition, I felt sure that Cynthiana wine required blending with *vinifera* to bring out its best. One April, the chance came to find out more on both counts.

Peter Machamer, wine critic at the time for the *Pittsburgh Post-Gazette*, helped me stage a tasting of eleven wines from Missouri and Arkansas. The palate panel included, among others, *Wine East* columnist Linda McKee and Owen Smith, who would go from a job at a Pennsylvania winery to Horton Vineyards, the Virginia producer of Norton wines mentioned in chapter 2. (Smith, more recently, moved on to a winery in Israel's Golan Heights; before landing at Phillips in California.)

I baked spicy zucchini lasagna and smoked two chickens for the wine to wash down, and we assembled at my Pittsburgh home. I knew most of the wines from travels around Missouri, and Peter had gotten interested during repeated visits to a friend in Kansas City who had a full cellar of Cynthiana and Norton wines. Mike Gonze, owner of the Pittsburgh importer-distributor Dreadnought Wines, had never tasted a wine called by either name. Smith and McKee had tasted only the Norton wine from Stone Hill, the winery which during the 1960s had resuscitated everyone's interest in the variety.

The most apparent conclusion from the tasting was that a real grab-bag of vinification methods were in use. Trying to distinguish between the two closely related varieties proved to be preposterous. A couple of winemakers had opted for a full-bodied, tannic, intensely flavored style in which maceration lasted probably for more than two weeks. Curtis Bourgeois, of Bourgeois Vineyards in Columbia, Missouri, had veered far afield, turning in a Cote-du-Rhone weight of wine meant to be drunk within two years of release. The other seven wines lay roughly along a continuum between the two styles.

The experience led McKee to comment in *Wine East's* July-August 1992 issue that "stylistic differences in the winemaking may be more important than whether the grape is a Norton or a Cynthiana."

A 1988 Norton (with 20 percent Chambourcin) from O'Vallon Winery in southwestern Missouri had the power and brawn without the abrasive tannins of a young Chateauneuf-du-Pape. Its concentrated flavor and flamboyant toffee-barnyard smell had delighted me months earlier when I tasted it at the winery, and I still loved it. (Some others thought its bouquet was out-of-bounds.)

The 1989 from Heinrichshaus Winery near St. James, Missouri, had mouth-watering bacon and coconut nuances and brambly, Zinfandel-like fruit, while a 1986 Cynthiana from Montelle Vineyards, near Augusta, Missouri, was astonishing, with beautifully focused cherry-candy fruit. It enlarged my ideas greatly of what a well-made Cynthiana wine could be.

McKee would call it a "delightful wine with a somewhat floral nose, strawberry, plum and coffee flavors, and a long wonderful finish."

After the tasting, a few of us gathered on the back porch, watching the chicken-fire embers die and enjoying the warm weather. As often happens, the panelists talked about wine and drank beer. "I couldn't believe the finish on that Montelle," said Owen, sipping his palate-cleansing Pilsener. "That was a six-year-old wine, and it was aging beautifully. It showed no signs of not going on for quite a while."

"Yeah, it was definitely hanging together," said Machamer, surprised, and echoing a point that many had wondered about: do Norton wines age? There was that '86 Montelle, and also an '87 from Montelle's Coyote Crossing Vineyard that was mature and also very good, slightly lighter than the other bottling but with glossy fruit and a deft mark of oak. The development of both Montelle wines suggested that the others stood to be excellent still at six to eight years. Most were three- or four-year-old releases. Machamer in his column the following week declared all of them "really interesting and often very good."

Stone Hill's entry, the 1990, was declared "off" by everyone – something had gone wrong: perhaps the cork had let in air. I had heard the wine described admirably by other trustworthy sources. The oldest wine, a 1976 Mount Pleasant Winery Cynthiana from Augusta, was jumping with smells and flavors – all bizarre and unattractive. Tasters were divided in their hypotheses. The wine came from Mount Pleasant's small planting in bench-lands along the Missouri River, but the vineyard had been grubbed out in the early '80s. I knew age wasn't the problem.

I knew from talking with Lucien Dressel, Mount Pleasant's owner way back in 1986. "We just found it impossible to grow," he had told me, discouraged especially because he liked other Cynthiana wines he'd tasted. Growing pains that plague every new wine region were palpable at Mount Pleasant in the mid-'80s. "Cynthiana's a vigorous plant anyway, but they just wrapped themselves up in knots in that rich soil," Dressel had said. He confessed that wines made from his grapes in the '70s were marred by horrible vegetal aromas.

Excessive vigor has a smell – of green, unripe grapes; weeds come to mind. With overly vigorous growth, the plant's energy is diverted from ripening fruit to producing vegetation. It's not an unheard-of problem in other parts of the world. Cabernet Sauvignon is a vigorous vine, too, and many red Bordeaux from the disastrous, cold 1977 vintage had the smell. Reds from the cooler areas of Washington state sometimes have the tell-tale stink, though this is less true than it was ten years ago. The weedy, briney green olive aroma used to be common in eastern U.S. red wines in all but the warmest years, though improved trellis systems have helped, as has letting the grapes hang longer – not being frightened by all of a ripening grape's enemies into picking before the crop is ripe.

"Creamed corn, asparagus," I had said at the tasting between bites of chicken and whiffs of the '76 Mount Pleasant. "It's like one of those bad cool-climate Cabernets from California from the early '80s. Cabernet from Monterey County used to smell like a bouquet of weed flowers."

On the back porch later, Linda McKee said: "Well, a person has one wine from Norton like this, and they may never come back."

She was right. The wine should never have been released, and I was a little puzzled why Mount Pleasant would have supplied it from its own reserves. I was also thinking how such a clunker can affect a winery's reputation years after a single wine is sold and forgotten. I vowed to not forget the lesson.

We were about to call it a night, though it was tough to give up on the warm April air. "How'd you get Mount Pleasant to give you that '76?" I asked Peter.

"Oh no, they didn't give it. It's from my friend's cellar in Kansas City. He sent it just for fun."

"Be sure to thank him," said Owen, shuddering.

Mount Pleasant has re-introduced Cynthiana from a new, hilltop vineyard. I tasted the '93 at the winery in the November after its release. It was sleek and fruity, not at all vegetal, and two cases short of being sold out, said the counter person, at $17 a bottle.

Spring 1993

IT SO HAPPENED that I had planned a trip to California to visit friends about six weeks after my first blends with Pinot Noir and Cynthiana in January 1993. I was pretty impressed with myself. With a winery where I'd sell this libation just starting to take shape in my mind, some critical comment from wine people in California couldn't hurt, I figured.

When I boarded the plane at Pittsburgh International for a twelve-day visit, I carried my case of small 375-ml bottles of Cynthiana wine under one arm.

I arrived in northern California during a wild, glorious space between

Basement wine cellar, Pittsburgh, 1993.

Chateau Montelena, Calistoga, California, 1993.

the torrential rains that had broken a long drought. Everything that makes the region so sumptuous was beginning to bloom. Wild mustard was jumping up in the aisles of the greening vineyards, and the soggy chapparral sprouted strange plants with day-glow colored flowers. Rain stopped the night I arrived and only warm, sunny days dawned wherever I went.

After three days with a friend in Sacramento, I borrowed his sleeping bag and his car and drove south and west on back roads into a forgotten sector of Napa County over the first line of tall hills out of Sacramento County. There was snow up there.

Then, descending the Napa hills back into spring along the the valley floor by way of the Silverado Trail, I drove north beyond Calistoga to visit Bo Barrett and Gerard Zanzanico and their crew at Chateau Montelena. When I worked there in 1986, I mostly cleaned things and moved things from one side of the building and back. I also gained my first appreciation for vineyard work by driving a tractor for the picking crews. It wasn't glamorous, but it was an apprenticeship.

Bo, part of the family which owns the winery and vineyards, is a savvy winemaker who has since received a string of commendations from the most important critics in the world for his Cabernet Sauvignon wines. It is hard to imagine more praise might be possible. Down-to-earth Bo had hired me because he had never met anyone from Missouri. "Now my cousin," he had told me, "is from Montana."

Gerard, the assistant winemaker, is a New York City native, a musician, and a self-taught winemaker devoted to his work but free of it at the same time. I worked a lot under his supervision. One day, I almost took his arm off by accidentally starting a piece of equipment with him partly inside. Fortunately for both of us, Gerard was always thinking.

Between the winemaker and his cellar crew of six others, counting me in 1986, Montelena for twenty-five years has made heady, often distinctive wines full of savage California-style fruit and minerally scents. Their estate-bottled Cabernet epitomizes the variety's possibilities for hot-climate wines.

For my part, I had found a delicious 1980 Montelena Chardonnay buried under plonk in a midwestern grocery store bin, and knowing Montelena's red wines by reputation, and being out of a permanent job, I had written Bo a letter asking for an apprenticeship job. Luckily, I was never too broke to buy a good bottle of wine. My mate at the time was finishing medical school, so I figured she wouldn't miss me for a few months anyway.

The only regret I have about working at Montelena is that I didn't spend enough time in the vineyard. If I had, I would likely have realized earlier on that wine was a product of the farm. A lot of people have said that good wine is made in the vineyard, and nowadays I thoroughly appreciate the saying. At that time, though, in 1986, I had not grown beyond an interest in wine – in the part of winemaking that goes on in the cellar.

My spring 1993 visit was my first return since working in Napa Valley. When I pulled up at the winery, Bo was in the lab holding a vial of wine to the window. He happily wisked took me away to his new house in a long canyon near the vineyard to show me where he was planting Sangiovese. He had smart plans for a "five-year Cabernet" blended with Sangiovese and maturing in half the time of his regular "reserve"-class Cabernet.

Back to the winery. We tasted from barrels for a while, then he and Gerard shuttered the tasting room and we worked the line: eight or nine vintages of reds and recent releases of their wonderfully old-fashioned Chardonnay – made in large tanks rather than small barrels and finished in a uniquely rich style – full of pineapple, pear, and papaya decadence that is oddly delicate all at once. Barrel-fermenting is an Old World technique that is much more time-consuming because small 53- to 55-gallon oak barrels are used instead of stainless steel tanks holding thousands of gallons.

Like tropical-flavored Chardonnay from ultra-ripe fruit, California pioneered the use of stainless steel tanks in the last half-century. More recently, trends moved away from this equipment for quality white wine, so that now Montelena's has become an unusual type of Chardonnay. In that crazy California way, "old-fashioned" is about twenty years old.

Equally subversive, by Old World (Burgundian) standards, much of California is too hot for Chardonnay, so the grape loses too much acidity before it is ripe. However, in California, the extra ripening also piles on guava and mango flavors that are rare for White Burgundy. "I could never see the logic in our situation," as Bo explains, "of adding acids at harvest, like just about everybody does in California, then putting the wine through malolactic, which takes away acidity. It also takes away fruit, which is why people like our style in the first place. We want to keep all the fruit in.

"Now everybody is barrel-fermenting, like the French always did, to add complexity and improve mouth-feel, but we have plenty of fruit and body and complexity already.

"Our philosophy, right or wrong, is 'More of Everything.'"

Right or wrong, corks were flying the day I visited. Bo opened the 1985 Cabernet, a wine I had helped make and the first vintage in which Bo had elected to leave all of the richest, strongest press wine out. Upon release of the '85 Cabernet, Robert Parker, in his *Wine Advocate,* scored it a 98, raving about its muscular balance and aging potential.

Of course I had tasted it many times in barrel when I was there, and I was part of the panel that made the decision about which barrels made the final "cut." Eight years, however, had transformed it into a maturing adult. Not all of Robert Parker's ravings stand the test of time, but he was right on the money about the '85 Montelena. It knocked me back from the counter, so long, strong and brilliant was its spirit. One can taste the inner earth in that wine, the minerally edge from the region's volcanic soil is so powerful.

Early on in the session, while opinions could be trusted, I had produced my little half-bottle of blended Cynthiana. Bo and Gerard sniffed and gulped, and Bo pronounced, "Yum, hey, that's good swill.

"What grapy fruit. Good weight, a little jamminess."

Leaving full of satisfaction and Montelena goodness, I called my wife to check in and to boast about Bo's comment. "He said my wine had good jamminess," I explained.

"Good for you – good jamminess," she said, mockingly.

Off the pay phone, I settled down to a picnic dinner of grocer-roasted chicken, lettuces, and crusty bread, topped by a secluded napette in a vineyard along the Silverado Trail (a spot I had pioneered one night in 1986 when festivities ran long and crazy at Montelena). A cold night fell as I snaked up the Mayacamas hills for Santa Rosa. There, I shopped for provisions and headed into the Alexander Valley.

Suddenly, it was 1 in the morning. I found a side road concealed from the highway by a hill, and sank into my sleeping bag, enveloped in a bank of fog rising from the Russian River.

It was breezy and warm by breakfast at a truck stop in Healdsburg, and the rest of the day was consumed revisiting haunts in northern Sonoma and the Dry Creek Valley. The valley is so pretty and unpretentious, and one can barely discern the importance of wine by driving only the main roads. I had always had a thing for the region's Zinfandel, spending many an off-day in 1986 tooling around to tasting rooms and cellars.

One important place had opened since I'd left – Meeker Vineyards, which had become one of the valley's hot Zinfandel houses by the early '90s. I stopped there around 11 a.m., and found an assistant winemaker tidying up. We tasted their luscious cherry candy-flavored, lighter "2-year" Zin and my wine. "That's a wild one – never tasted anything like that, for sure," said the assistant who gave only his first name. "I'd like to show it to my boss. Trade you a big bottle for two of your little ones," he said.

At a wine store I knew in the area, which specializes in old vine California Zinfandels, I met the salesmen who had replaced the one I'd known. Pat stuck his nose over my Cynthiana and did a huge double-blink. "What is that?" he shrieked. "It's fantastic. I smell salty, smoky bacon and," – he stuck his nose back below the rim; dumbfounded, looked up at me – "and something . . ."

"I smell gingerbread," I said.

"Yeah, that is it. Christ, gingerbread. I can sell a few cases of this a month, easy."

I told him it was homemade, but that I'd get back to him in five years. "Well, I'll be gone by then," he said. "My girlfriend and I are starting a winery up in El Dorado.

"But I'll buy from you myself. Give me your address."

TEMPTING AS IT would be to leave out negative commentary on this California trip about my first Cynthiana wine, I can't. There simply wasn't any. I know it sounds absurd to insist that these accolades occurred for a wine made in my basement, largely from a Native American grape, but everywhere I went, people were dazzled. Friends liked the wine as well as strangers.

The most ringing endorsement came in Amador County when I visited Scott Harvey, who at the time was part-owner of Santino Winery and Grand Peré vineyard, the oldest Zinfandel plants in the world. (Harvey, too, has moved on, most recently to Folie á Deaux in Napa.) Bo Barrett had rec-ommended Harvey because Santino was experimenting with blends of odd Portuguese and Italian varieties. I also wanted to see Syrah, a grape nearly as vigorous in its growth habits as Cynthiana, being grown in a bush-like fash-ion without a trellis. I'd heard this "head-pruned" method was used for Syrah in Amador, and I was attempting to grow Cynthiana in the same way. I thought maybe I could learn a trick or two.

Only problem was – dah! – there were no growing lessons to be had, it being the dormant season. (A friend with whom I had arranged to do some editing work asked me recently if I am a "detail person." I told him I was good at all the details I remembered.)

Well, despite my foolishness, there was still Scott Harvey. He is one of California's most charismatic, devil-may-care personages. When I walked in to Santino Winery, he was seated behind the tasting bar talking on the phone about pallet jacks. I produced the little bottle from the inside pocket of my vest, tipped my head at it, and pointed a finger at him, then me. He continued the pantomime by smiling, nodding a grandiose affirmative, and pulling two glasses from below the counter as he continued talking.

As he got off the phone, he said: "And what he do we have here?"

I explained my business, told him how the wine was made, with what grapes, and asked if he had tasted many eastern red wines. I poured him a glass. "Can't stand 'em. I had a Pinot Noir or two from New York that was okay, but I think they're pretty horrible usually."

"You mean Konstantin Frank's Pinot, don't you?" I said, referring to Vinifera Wine Cellars in the the Finger Lakes of New York. "That's a great wine, the real Burgundy."

"Yeah," he said, shocked, "as a matter of fact I do."

Then he sniffed and tasted my wine, held my wine in his mouth, looked at me, and got up with my wine still in his mouth while motioning with one finger to his lips as in, "Don't say anything." At the door of an adjoin-ing room, he swallowed and said: "Say, come out here. There's a guy from Pennsylvania who brought in something you won't believe."

A woman, never introduced, came out and we all tasted the wine. She loved it. Scott Harvey said: "I'm gonna tell you, I've been waiting for some-one to come up with a wine like this from out East." I'll be gracious here and cut short his rhapsodizing, the full text of which I hurriedly scribbled down ten minutes later when I got to the car: "This is a very intelligent wine. It has that grape jelly sort of flavor – more a smell than a flavor – that is a reference point for a lot of customers because it is familiar. A dry wine that has this sort of aroma is a wine that can only be made in eastern America – a true regional specialty. It smells so good and grapy, like grape jam on your toast in the morning."

He wanted a case for his personal collection. I told him I wasn't "commercial" yet but arranged to trade a half-case, after I bottled in late summer, for an assortment of his wines.

Among the wines he sent was an experimental red blockbuster made mainly from the Portuguese Tinta Cáo that has stuck in my memory like fox fur. It was velvet. And it was roasted, with a tall glycerine miniscus much like a great Dão from Portugal.

After returning from California, I concluded that what I had learned reinforced the logic of making the blend I liked. Pinot Noir has great advantages because it has become a regular producer in the East during the last decade; though it is known for capriciousness in setting a crop, several New York wineries grow the grape and make wine from it every year. Clonal variation is a problem gradually being solved as the best and hardiest clones are singled out.

Vinifera Wine Cellars in Hammondsport issues a delicate, flowery wine from the clone that the late eastern *vinifera* specialist Dr. Konstantin Frank brought from Europe in the early 1960s. It has as pretty a Burgundy soul as I've come across. The 1991 made me paw the air, it was so delicious and fragile and full of bouncy fruit. I called Fred Frank, the son who took over for his father, and begged him to tell me where to find more. It was sold out, but I've bought each vintage since. (Even the '92, a famously bad year in our region, was fine.)

The West Coast (and much of Burgundy nowadays) specializes in bold, gripping expressions of the Pinot grape which can be excellent but are hardly traditional. Great Burgundy can verge on the powerful, but in its heart it's an introvert, from cold climate grapes with testy acidity. It offers round, textured fruit by impression, wound around a medium-bodied frame. One reads Chekhov with a glass of Burgundy; you watch TV with most California Pinot.

If it's fat and gooey, it's either from California or from Burgundy producers who rely on heavy additions of sugar during fermentation (or heavier wines from the Mediterranean region) to increase body and alcohol. Such Burgundy is mainly sold outside France. By contrast, Oregon was highly touted for its Burgundy-like breakthroughs with Pinot Noir, now twenty years past, but as these wines have aged the bulk of critical opinion is pointing to a need for much refinement still.

To be fair, that is occurring in Oregon, thanks to innovations in the vineyard especially – especially new trellising techniques that give the vine more room to spread its foliage in rich soils. This tends to refine the wine's flavors. (In poor soils, the closer spacing of vines common in Europe has a similar effect.)

The single best way to make better wine, Americans on the West Coast know, is to grow better grapes. In the East, such commitment has made fewer inroads.

As a "blender" *vinifera*, Pinot offers advantages mainly in more northerly growing areas in the East that have lower humidity. There it can be raised as successfully or more so than other red *vinifera* (though Cabernet Franc is certainly a rival). But Pinot Noir, alone among all red grapes grown in the East – hybrid, native, or *vinifera* – can make a wine naturally soft on the palate. This makes it especially valuable in cool climate wines, which tend to the sharply acidic. In addition, northeastern America has clay-rich soils. Many *vinifera* don't succeed on such soils, and the best Burgundian soil is limestone-based.

A chief concern with *vinifera* is how they survive cold winters. For decades – centuries, depending on when you start counting – it was thought that winter cold prevented *vinifera* from being grown in eastern America. But in the last twenty years, evidence has poured in that other factors are more important than cold (such as the soil's PH and its potassium reserves). Pinot Noir growers in the Finger Lakes – the Niagara region in Ontario also has shown its suitability for Pinot – produced about half of their regular crop after winter temperatures fell as low as -24 once in the 1990s, so Pinot's winter hardiness is as good as any French hybrid. This is the main French realization of recent decades: many hybrids are cold-hearty, but so are a few *vinifera*, which seem universally to make better wine. So, planting hybrids makes no sense.

Pinot Noir is now preferred in several districts in northern France, Switzerland, Germany, and Austria because of its superior cold-heartiness. It is a cool-weather grape, whether planted in Burgundy, Alsace, the Carneros section of Napa Valley, Oregon, Pennsylvania, or Tyrolian Italy.

I corresponded about Pinot's unappreciated versatility with Gerald Asher, the *Gourmet* wine critic, after his magazine column about Missouri wine. He especially liked a New World role for Burgundy's aristocrat.

"Pinot Noir," he pointed out, "is rarely thought of as a blending grape, if only, I imagine, because its own taste is so delicate that other varieties are never used to supplement it. But that's no reason why it wouldn't be useful the other way 'round." Yet very few U.S. or Australian wineries are doing it. In fact, Asher knew only that the Frescobaldi family in Tuscany uses about 20 percent Pinot Noir in their "Pomino" red wine. "They've been doing it since some time in the 19th century."

Quite a few wineries in out-of-the-way parts of France use Pinot in blends, and a handful of California producers use a little in non-traditional ways, but certainly there are no regional table wines of worldly importance from Pinot Noir blends.

While attempts to make *grand cru* from 100 percent Pinot in North America will continue on a limited basis, blended wines from Pinot are of more use in more parts of the East than other highly prized red European grapes.

SPRING WAS A LONG TIME in coming to my vineyard in 1993. The last two weeks of March and the first two in April were sloshy and nasty, which is fairly typical for western Pennsylvania. I recorded in my journal that the area had not had "three consecutive sunny days since last fall. Saturday, the 17th, I was out there and it may as well have been January 17: 40 m.p.h. wind, snow pellets bouncing off my coveralls."

We seldom experience the warmish, showery spring weather of yore, and instead go straight from chilly and damp to warm and muggy. Nineteen ninety-three was an exception, but of a different kind. By May 1, the rain and snow of only two weeks earlier were forgotten; temperatures zoomed into the upper 80s and low-90s. Everything looked like mid-summer. The vineyard work was hot in an almost tropical lushness. Coming so early after the long winter, the warmth gave me great joy.

The weeds were rampant, but I had prepared myself with a tool that I'd special-ordered from a professional landscaping supply house. Seeing me flailing away, Lou, Mrs. Weaver's son, stopped by one afternoon. Relations were not chummy between us – he still took every chance he had for snide comments – but we did at least say hello to one another.

"What's you got there?" he asked. "A big ole hoe? Man, that thing'll do some damage."

I registered this as his first positive comment about my efforts on the farm.

Directly, a woman came down the hill with two mutt puppies clinging to her shoulders. The woman stood near Lou as we talked and the puppies crawled all over her. We talked on and on, but Lou never introduced us.

Finally I introduced myself, producing a quizzical, befuddled look on her face. I asked her what her name was.

"Cathy," she blurted, dipping her head to avert my gaze. She was probably 35 years old but had the manner of a child. I thought, perhaps, she was mildly retarded. Her relationship to Lou, a good ten years her elder, was also not clear.

He spoke to her as one would a kid sister – more about her than to her. "Cathy's got some new puppies," Lou said. "Cathy sure likes animals. Cathy's always hanging around the animals."

He would look approvingly at her, and she'd look down; otherwise, Cathy acknowledged no one, it seemed. They had to get moving, Lou said. "Yeah, we're going over to Rogers, Ohio, over to the flea market there."

"Last week, I sold $35 worth of hot sauce. People were buying it a dollar a bottle."

Mrs. Weaver had told me that Lou was making his living by selling things at flea markets around the area. He had bought a ramshackle turquoise house trailer at an auction, and installed it on the hill by the barn. I noticed there was electric going in, but no running water.

He was spraying the apple trees, though he never did prune them to increase their production and, according to Mrs. Weaver, planned to harvest apples in the fall and sell those at the markets. Looked like Rogers was a regular venue for him.

I realized then that Cathy was the person I'd seen earlier with a head and shoulders stuck in through the door of the pig pen. I had seen her lower torso when I drove past to park in the barn lot.

Lou had bought a pig not much smaller than a Honda Civic and had somehow wedged the huge animal into a utility shed not much bigger than a Honda Accord. I had looked in the week before to see the sow on her side, and the suckling pigs barely able to all feed at once. I mean space was cramped.

The days of capital investment were history at Weaver Farm; now it was down to whatever income could be sucked from what was left. Barn siding fell off in a storm, not to be replaced, so the weather poured in and rotted the century-old floor. Wind whipped the equipment barn's aluminum door off and out into the field; no one picked it up. Mrs. Weaver's roof leaked; so throw a tarp over it, maybe it'll go another year. It was sad to see, and one sees it all over the countryside in our region; people with enormous paid-for farms, but no clue how to make a living from their land.

But back to hoeing. My tool was a long-handled "grape hoe," American-made, with a lightweight ash handle and an extra-wide drop-forged blade. In large vineyard operations, the preference is for an awkward, hydraulic scraper contraption (also called a "grape hoe," though swung hydraulically) on a tractor that I've seen take out vines instead of weeds occasionally. On big farms, money-makers, the capital goes into machinery instead of humans.

Maybe it had to be that way, for all I knew. What did I know about big-time farming?

A good hand hoe, I did quickly learn, cut the weeding time on a 190-foot-long vineyard row, for a little fellow like me, from the ninety minutes I'd spent with the common hardware store item to just over thirty minutes.

I weeded the ten-row vineyard twice before May 15, claiming as my own in the hot and still grueling process an archetypal image of a figure swinging a medieval tool. Hundreds of times I heard its ritual report: *"Whoosh k-chew, whoosh k-chew, whoosh k-chew."* I still use the hoe. The sound forms a wood-cut of the activity, a block-print on my brain pan.

One evening in late April, while hoeing, head down to avoid the glare of early spring's southerly sun, I heard what sounded like canvas crackling in a heavy wind. I paused for an instant and the sound grew louder. Just as I looked up, a lone Canadian geese flew out of the sun only 20 feet over my head.

The majestic bird passed so close in its course over the hillside that I realized the canvas-like rippling I had heard was the gristle in the bird's wings as they flapped – an event made even more incredible by the fact that I was alerted to the sound's very existence only a few nights earlier by a character's experience with a water bird in Walker Percy's novel, *The Movie-goer*. The character also reported the sound of canvas crackling.

A journal entry of May 7 says: "Saw flying banana goldfinches and big hawk birds soaring over all. I chop the weeds, I hoe the soil, I prune the plants, I handle them over and over. In the wine from this land, I have to wonder, will you taste the hand?"

Mid-June (from my journal)

> I've been out there three times this month just watering, with 5 gallons buckets from the spring down the hill. The aisles have inch-wide, cracked-open rivulets. Last night, I was there until 9:30, mowing and tying and pulling weeds. One thing I've noticed is that the more I work on the vines, and just be around them, the more I want to go back.
>
> Saturday I was up at 6 a.m., on the hill by 7:15, and working until 8 p.m. I came home tired to my core – I could feel fatigue in my bones and organs – and I swear I could have gotten up and gone right back out there the next day.

"How can you be in such a good mood?" Nadine would ask when I'd come home at 10 o'clock and we'd still manage to have an evening of bounteous food and fun. "I don't see how you're holding your head up."

There are few feelings so full as when my head hits the pillow after a day in the sun and wind on that hill of grapes. As I drift off, the thrill I feel is enlarged by the surety of being so bound to sweet earth.

One of those nights, however, as I lay in bed and great fluffy balls of cotton pressed against me on all sides and my brain half-sorted soft orange thoughts of the day, a memory suddenly flashed up that I had not had in, I counted up, more than twenty-five years. In fact, perhaps I'd not "thought" of the event, actually, since the days right after it happened.

It had been such a non-event really, but now, mulling over it, I couldn't keep my eyes closed.

Certain combinations were occurring – certain possibilities. I sat up, wide-awake.

I had been no more than 8 or 9 years old. My mother and I were visiting her seldom-seen friends in the country, and an older man at the house (I don't remember his connection exactly) had led me to the garden and showed me how to pull a carrot up by its green hair. He yanked one himself, then let me do one. Once he rubbed the dirt off mine, he said to bite it. I remember his wide-eyed smile when I tasted the carrot, my first taste of anything straight from a garden.

It seemed, when I thought about the event now, that I remembered being stunned by the flavor: its sweetness, the faint taste of soil, its honest, crisp flesh. Sitting in bed, I recalled the crunchy sound I made chomping it. I could almost feel it in my mouth.

Later, after we'd left the place, I had asked my mother if we could grow some carrots in our yard, or at least, could we buy fresh carrots instead of canned or frozen ones? She laughed and lit another smoke from the dashboard lighter. Fresh vegetables are so old-fashioned, she said.

I swear I thought I could remember that my question had made her nervous – how she fumbled with the cigarette lighter; or maybe it was the awkward silence that followed her reply. I could remember something like that, something that made me think of her actions in that way: she associated fresh vegetables with something far bigger than their flavor or fine flesh. And she never really answered my question.

Nadine rustled but did not awake as I got out of bed. Outside, with a glass of Ruby Port – Christian Brothers, cheap stuff but potable – I sat on the lip of the porch, chest hunched over my knees, and sipped the glass continuously as a big blade on a long shaft worked the thoughts in my brain into fresh heaps.

I had been reading a lot. New things. I had skipped the English Lake Poets of the 1800s but revisited Thoreau in a big way, scavenged around for John Muir's more obscure work, and read biographies about them as well. I read a few nineteenth century stories by John Burroughs, and those of modern writers such as Barry Lopez and Wendell Berry. I also happened upon the 1950s' books of Leonard Hall, a Missouri farmer known in his day as "the state's most popular outdoors writer." Hall wrote what I think is still the best one-paragraph critical description of Thoreau's body of work ever penned. He also wrote that the workings of the world of animals and plants were alien to most people, even in the '50s, so the joys of engaging once again "with the land" are difficult to communicate because so few in the audience have shared the experience.

Was it true, I asked myself, that communication with others about what I was learning and feeling was hard, and would always be hard, because so few modern people have had similar experiences with the land? There was evidence to the contrary, I thought. The woman at Borders Books in Pittsburgh had told me once that titles in the "Nature and Animals" section were among the best sellers. I can certainly confirm that their stock turns over regularly. Of course Thoreau's *Walden* is considered one of the classics. I had read it first in some basic college course – maybe even in high school. What interested me that night, hunched up on the porch, was whether Thoreau's message had been heard. Even if, as Hall said, modern people no longer engage enough with the land, I had a hard time believing that anything but a solid majority of Americans supported an improvement in our society's overall relationship with the natural environment. That much, I thought, I knew for sure.

So, as the narrator in Percy's novel puts it, "What do you seek – God? you ask with a smile."

I went inside for another Christian Brothers. There was another experience, only a few days before – on one of those freakishly hot spring days.

In Pittsburgh during the mid-1990s, every time the temperature reached 90 degrees or so, the area faced what the U.S. Environmental Protection Agency called an "Ozone Action Day." The ozone produced mainly from natural humidity and car exhaust reaches such high levels in the atmosphere that the air is dangerous "to young children and the elderly" (as if it's harmless to healthy, middle-aged people). This severe smog condition, occurring because the area did not meet the EPA clean air standards and because Pennsylvania took its sweet time to draft measures to gain compliance, was widely reported in the media. The state could have lost its federal highway funds if non-compliance continued.

So, what could have explained the response of a filling station clerk when I asked why his station didn't have one of those round, $5 ozone shields on its pump?

"Yeah, they're threatening to make us use them," he said, "but so far we've been able to get around it."

He had said it as if I were bound to be on his side, and I assume he said it that way because he found that most people were.

Am I to believe that this man never heard of Hank Thoreau? Does he not want a healthier environment?

It was 1:30 in the morning, and there I was, on the porch wondering if I were the only one who saw a connection between Thoreau and ozone shields on gas pumps.

Yet, I must admit to undertaking the remainder of this communication without knowing if I fumble for questions that most everyone else has already answered, or if I am in some essential way "untethered," free of the condition described by Thoreau in *The Maine Woods*, in which "he who rides and keeps to the beaten track studies the fences chiefly." I think of this question just about every hour as I go through just about every day. And so far, I keep wondering if I'll ever know any answers.

Summer and "Harvest" 1993

TO MY ASTONISHMENT, tiny green grapes replaced the flower petal caps that dropped off the blossoms on my two-year-old vines in June 1993. The hot but not-too-dry weather continued all summer, which blew by like a flash. The first vintage tallied about 70 pounds. It happened, according to my journal, on the 2nd Saturday of September 1993:

> Nadine and I had a little golden harvest, beneath a great fac-
> ing sunset, hearts pumping at the wonder of our own black
> bunches plunking in our baskets as we went down the rows.
> I knew I would hate to crush them up, to see the year end.
> Then I saw Nadine's crinkled cheeks, like ripe, rubbed
> peaches, and it was fall; the color was all around, on leaves
> and necks.

-five-

Early Winter 1993

ONE PART OF GRAPE-GROWING that I had looked forward to since I began reading about it ten-odd years ago was pruning. I enjoy outdoor winter work, and vines are pruned in cold weather. Every plant in the Scenery Hill vineyard had to be trimmed after the 1993 growing season, and it was my first time. So, I was as eager for the leaves to fall as I had been for them to appear in spring.

The eagerness was tinged with anxiety, because I didn't know if it would take me two days or two weeks. In western Pennsylvania, one never knows how many "outdoor work days" there will be once winter sets in. There might be one or two a week, but more typically the sun doesn't show for a fortnight at a time. Pittsburgh, statistically, has almost exactly the same number of cloudy days per year as Portland. Rain- or snow-free stretches are rare from early November through the end of April. I've also seen May masquerade as March.

The damp and cloudy winters are much like those in famous winegrowing parts of Europe, too. Pruning traditionally begins in November or early December in Europe. But in eastern America, a lot of vineyardists wait until late February or March so that if severe temperatures in mid-winter kill buds, where the coming year's growth is stored, more buds may be left on the vine once the bad weather has passed. The more buds one leaves, the more fruit the plant can produce.

Grape varieties vary tremendously in their tolerance of sub-zero weather, but Cynthiana, being a native of America's forests, is among the hardiest of all. The chance of a fierce winter didn't concern me much, so I felt safe in pruning early. Just about all outdoor winter work is improved by sun overhead, but it is especially welcome for pruning. Sun on the vine's canes makes them more elastic, easier to twist around on the trellis.

The trellis, it should be explained, supports the vines during the growing season when they are loaded with leaves and fruit. In fact, most of the sprawling branches one sees in a summertime vineyard are trimmed off after the growing season. The vine bears fruit only from buds on a cane, which is the wood formed each new growing season. All but those canes wanted for producing fruit in the following year are lopped off.

On Day 1, I pulled cheerily into Scenery Hill around 8 a.m., after the hour drive from the city. Although the sun had risen through partial clouds, it had them on the run when I arrived. A slight chance of rain was predicted, but I chanced it because at least the temperature was mild for December. Even on cloudy days, I figured, my first taste of pruning would be fun – so long as that wind wasn't whipping.

I pulled off my heavy top layers, and set to work – Year 2, Top Row, Plant 1, Cut 1.

The mental stimulation proved to be a blend of mathematics, geometry and a pleasing element of chance roughly comparable to, say, billiards. As with so many aspects of winegrowing, a balance had to be found between full concentration – decisions about each plant required due haste, there being a lot of wood to prune – and idle musing over the horse-head shape of a cloud, the bite in the breeze, or the pretty patina of cane wood.

Inspecting the wood of each plant, I found some canes not "hardened off" enough from their summer green to survive the coming winter. Cold weather had come suddenly that fall, and some canes were caught without their winter coats buttoned up. A gradual cool-down after leaf-fall, once the plant has pulled the nitrogen from the soil and finished manufacturing its winter bark, is ideal for the hardening of cane wood. The injured wood on Cynthiana's canes was blotchy and pale, sickly looking, and sometimes even slightly soft to the touch, instead of bright brown and armor-hard. Buds on damaged wood, I knew, were much more susceptible to severe cold – sometimes all the buds on an injured cane perish.

How well canes that are hardened off fare through the winter varies, but those that grew most rampantly during the season – winegrowers know them as "bull canes" – are not good candidates for keeping. Thick as they are, bull canes lack the inner mettle for surviving extreme cold. They're like bullies. Learn to spot the bull cane; never count on a bull cane.

Six or seven plants down the top row, I noticed clouds streaming thickly overhead. The sun, now, was on the run, the sky a greying pewter.

My progress did not feel quick enough; in fact, I'd say I was as insecure about my task as any pruner working that season, I'd bet, anywhere in the world, though explaining the steps in the abstract is fairly easy. On each plant, I had to calculate the canes' position for supporting hanging fruit in the following year. Yet, the pruner tries not only to predict the future, but also to recreate the past. Based on how much the spindly branches were bunched together, I estimated the canopy's density and the sun's penetration: a cane with buds hidden by overhanging foliage early in the growing season wasn't a good bet for the coming year, because shading reduces carbohydrate buildup, making the vine less apt to bear fruit the next year. By about the end of tenth week of the growing season – by late June in most regions – buds for the following year are formed, and their exposure to direct sun during their period of formation determines which buds have the potential to bear fruit the next year.

The pruner must play shrewd hunches about how many buds to leave for fruiting, each vine having personal levels of vigor and shading, while he also tries to achieve rough uniformity throughout the vineyard so that crops can be predicted, supported, and ripened at roughly the same time year after year.

Then there are the invalids. Some plants in any vineyard are always hobbling along. Winter cold damages some, so that whole sections of the plant are stunted or dead. In eastern America, at least two main trunks are usually trained up from the ground. Cracked or diseased trunks must be sawed off and new trunks started. Removing a trunk basically cuts in half the vine's fruiting potential for the following season, and restoring a new trunk (or cordon) on the trellis, in position to again bear a full crop, takes at least two full years.

Sometimes, if a plant looked strong enough, I left the usual number of buds on the healthy canes and also saved the stunted section, to see if the plant could overcome on its own whatever ailed it. I may sound confident now, but I just figured that adjustments could always be made later; if a damaged cane didn't produce growth from its buds in spring – "bud out" as growers say – I could remove it then. (Once spring comes and the leaves are growing, I would find out, attention must be given in individual doses, which is very time-consuming. Spring is the busiest season in a well-run vineyard.)

Pruning, the reader may discern, is a hyper-human endeavor, so miscalculations and wrong choices occur. Mistakes cause crop reductions in summer and the plant becomes unbalanced on one side, often leading to pruning headaches and further loss of crop for a couple or three years afterward.

I may sound learned now, but after maybe 90 minutes in December 1993, when I stood up to stretch my arms and back, twist my neck muscles, and inspect the sky I found that I'd finished only nine vines. Do the math: I had 300 vines to prune.

Little matter.

Fifteen minutes later, I was completely down, hunkered against a tree in the nearby apple orchard, as rain, hail, ice pellets mixed with snow, and eventually all snow swept across the hillside in lusty waves. Tree limbs danced wildly. Leaves and brush blew by. Under the apple tree, I lowered my hat to an angle where I could watch what was happening but keep the flying moisture off my glasses.

The wind howled in a way that made me fear a December tornado until, sickeningly, the temperature started down, sliding in five minutes toward pure winter. Water balls then rolled off the hat brim and onto my curled up denim knees, and a bit later, onto my nose, down the face and onto my lightweight absorbent jacket. I dropped my head fully, spread my knees, and watched drip after drip after drip splash on grass blades between my legs. It was some sad-sack siesta scene.

As a pruner and a man working outside on the brittle fringe of winter, I realized, I was not prepared.

I bolted for the car, vowing to invest in waterproof outerwear before coming back ever again. When I looked back the last time, lacy snow patches were forming on the weed bunches, and everywhere water dripped. December raw infested the place.

Recuperating that night, a carafe of ruby-colored claret nearby, I was drawn to the account of a pruner's day by Oliver Mayo, in his *The Wines of Australia* (1986). I had read it years ago, before I was a pruner myself, and it had gone right over my head. Mayo's sketch starts with the farmer ten minutes out of bed, "hunched up at the end of a quarter of a mile of gnarled bushes, fifteen or twenty canes rising a yard from each one's five stumpy arms. After half an hour, his spare hand is blue with cold, and his nose, acting like a condenser, runs steadily."

Then the rain begins, and he curses and pulls his cap down closer over his eyes. Rain drips into them, and he cuts the fleshy part of his thumb just a little and curses again.

The rain is a light drizzle, but coming from the East it will get worse. He raises his eyes momentarily and looks across the valley to the light grey gums above the vines. They merge into the gusting drizzle. He takes a bottle of raisin liqueur muscat from the deep pocket of his greatcoat and swigs, a big mouthful. Then he bends to his task. Another hour and the sodden greatcoat weighs a ton and there is a minor torrent down his spine, where the pleats open as he moves, and there is only one thickness of khaki felt. He sighs and plods on.

After a lunch of canned tomato soup, Mayo writes, and the donning of dry clothes and "a plastic raincoat with a rip under one arm," the pruner "plods out again, but the storm has arrived and he cannot prune where he cannot see a foot. The midweek movie is Ray Milland in 'The Lost Weekend,' enlivened by crackles and flashes of lightning."

I didn't have a quarter-mile of vines, but it still took me nearly three full days to prune my vineyard in 1993 – three days spread out over portions of six because the weather was so lousy. December that year was hideous. I didn't have a greatcoat, but I did get the torrent down my spine (even with the rain gear), and I didn't have raisin liqueur muscat, but I want to take this opportunity to thank the Austin Nichols Distillery Co. for Wild Turkey American bourbon.

TRAVAIL IN THE FIELD, though, could not dampen my spirits about the '93 vintage. At two months old, I thought I had something truly memorable. The season, after all, had been nearly ideal, with above average temperatures, and below average rainfall. Again, I had picked Cynthiana in Virginia, and the wines were fruity and had lots of juicy appeal.

Right before the new year, I made blends with my Virginia-grown Cynthiana and wine from other varieties I picked in the Lake Erie area. I decided to keep my little dab of "estate-grown" Cynthiana separate, at least until spring. I knew a guy in Missouri who had made an astounding wine from two-year-old Cynthiana vines. It happens.

A friend came over, and we did the mixing. The red wines were already delicious. We agreed that we could sit right down, like bears around a beehive, and have a jolly time – with, maybe, gorgonzola cheese and walnuts, a rustic bread, and say, a pomegranate.

The '93 Cynthiana-Pinot Noir-Chambourcin-Vidal wine, my second vintage of the blend, was, commented my friend Philip, "unbelievably delicate." There was an avalanche of fruit – strawberries and cranberries, some elderberry. "It's like you could close your eyes and think you're tasting a white wine," he marveled. "But then there's all those red berries."

"I want it to be so delicate that it seems you could just break it in two," I said to him.

I felt such tenderness about the wines I made that year. Awed at getting my own vines through the early summer drought, at seeing so many bunches in only the plants' second year, at them turning blue in early August, at the hot ripening spell at the end, and then at collecting the fruits of my labors, wine's creative spiral knocked me out: I had transformed awe into something living and soulful, to be drunk and returned to the earth.

People have celebrated the winter season in late December for many a millennia, with wine as the medium much of that time, and I was sodden with the spirit that year.

It was all new to me. Wine traps time and space in a bottle, you know.

All through the season, I had tied plants up to the wires, hacked and scratched and shaved the earth – hundreds of hours, nearly every weekend, golden tan by early June; mountain sunset after mountain sunset after a full workday in the city. On some full moon nights, I even worked by moonlight until 10 or 10:30. Sudden storms left me drenched and shivering in the car on the way home a few other times.

I felt so vulnerable so often, awed by a new appreciation of how miniscule I was in time and space, and by how I valued everything around me so much more. The inevitable result is humility.

What came from my mind and hands in the cellar was sweet and fragile. I wanted no bombast.

(The '93 got prettier and prettier, with Jolly Rancher candy fruit, a silky, melt-away finish, and a demure personality for which comparisons didn't come easy. The blend and the long maceration of the skins made a Cynthiana wine like no other, closer to Burgundy than to Bordeaux, with a roundness on the palate that left most people asking for more. I write parenthetically because the wine was still young when it seemed to stop improving in mid-1996. Maybe it's in an idle state, and it's too early to say if it will be a pirouetting beauty a decade from now. Or, as with many other wines, maybe since it has stopped improving, decline is not far off. I truly don't know. The fact is, good wine can be young or old, but all great wine must age.)

Later in Winter, Early 1994

THE RAPTURE of vintage time died abruptly in mid-January 1994, during the coldest temperatures ever recorded in much of northeastern America.

In a half-dozen Arctic nights, all I could do was look south out the picture window toward Scenery Hill and fret at how 2-year-old plants could possibly survive. It reached -24 degrees one night; four other times, it went to -15 or colder. There was a lot of snow.

As soon as I could drive around, on a sunny Sunday afternoon when the thermometer crept to a steamy +2, I made my way south to Scenery Hill. Mrs. Weaver appeared at her door when I drove up, so I got out to check if she was okay.

Inside, it was her and the woman Cathy, huddled together in the kitchen with all four burners going on the stove and young adult pups running everywhere. I counted seven, plus two cats.

Lou had gone to Florida to see his daughter, Mrs. Weaver said. "I guess it got too cold for him in that trailer. The wind blows up there."

"Got too cold for you up there, too, I imagine," I said to Cathy, not really thinking.

She didn't look up. "Oh, Cathy stays down here," Mrs. Weaver said, "Cathy's better off down here."

The exact Lou-Cathy alignment was more than I needed to know, I decided, and asked no more. I had to get out of that house, where it seemed that conditions had worsened since fall.

But first I couldn't help but look around. Mrs. Weaver murmured that she needed to wash her floors, which were smeared with brown stains, out-right mud, and mud and hairball wads. The place was steaming hot, and the smell of dog, all-purpose organic decay, and dog feces crowded out nearly all other vapors. Cans, dust-and-grease caked jars, aluminum tins and ancient, greasy cooking utensils choked every counter or other horizontal surface in the kitchen.

Southwestern Pennsylvania is, according to the federal government's Appalachian Commission, part of Appalachia, and Mrs. Weaver could have been a spokesperson. For me, having grown up in the Ozarks, hers were not alien ways (the complex imprint of poor education, physical labor, and isolation of life in rugged hill country being, perhaps, a common thread); I often felt at home with Mrs. Weaver. Being around her reminded me of visiting Grandma as a child. As an adult, I was fascinated and repelled.

I wondered what Cathy thought, and where, in fact, she did stay. "You need anything?" I said to them.

"No, we'll make it," Mrs. Weaver said, sincere and sweet as pie.

"Say hello to Lou when he makes it back," I said, pulling the door shut to the frigid, refreshing wind.

Happy to get outside, I veered for the vineyard, with shovel, thermometer, and Wild Turkey in tow.

The sun was as blinding as oblivion; ice runs 4 feet long and several inches thick clung to the sides of trees, while tiny icicles dangled from limbs, tinkling on the wind. Snow drifts were waist-deep in the fence rows. I stopped frequently to admire the bleak other-worldliness – how did plants, much less animals survive this sort of climate? – while struggling from car to

Dorothy Weaver, Scenery Hill, 1994.

hillside across 200 yards of crusty snow.

In the vineyard, I shoveled away at the base of the plants, down, down, through nearly 3 feet of snow. There, to my astonishment, I found the earth not even frozen, with temperatures hovering in the low 30s. The snow had come early and fast, and the vines had been buried in a deep insulating pile since the first polar currents had swept down.

I can say this much for the unlikely viticultural belt that I call home: on the best sites, we routinely have a 185-day growing season between spring and fall frosts; plenty of sun in summer with – again, on the best sites – only moderate humidity build-up because of how the air rolls downhill; and when it gets cold enough to damage the vines, it seems always to snow heavily right before.

Trudging uphill back to my car was, for an out-of-shape winter convalescent, an Everest-like expedition. But I did so believing the young vines were snugly insulated in the snowpack. It looked like they would be just fine.

A FEW WEEKS LATER, Nadine and I went to Europe on vacation.

Enough of my Cynthiana blend had clarified in the top few inches of the glass tanks that I could siphon some off to take along. I wrapped a half-dozen small bottles in sweaters and bluejeans and stuffed them in my bag.

Much of just about everything I accomplish happens at the last second, so, with one exception, I contacted no European vintners before we left. We knew we were going to Paris, and through Provence and Tuscany by car, but when Nadine and I travel we keep advance planning to a strict minimum. A vacation from time is what we are after as much as anything.

I guessed we'd wind up at a winery or two, and I took the wine along figuring it was a great chance to collect more critical commentary.

We drove south from Paris, through Burgundy on Sunday backroads where hardly anything stirs in Catholic France, across the Alps and into northern Italy.

This visit, too, was sun-blessed. Rosemary and thyme were flowering when we pulled up at the villa we had rented near Lucca, an hour west of Florence. Nadine had spent the summer of 1981 in Lucca as a college student, and so we thought it would be a good place to stay and launch day trips. She still knew a few people there.

The Lucchese air was heavy with the smoke of burning vine cuttings. Vineyards on our estate looked out on a valley and a set of low mountains, south toward Chianti. This is a wine district of local importance, the Montecarlo appellation being the most prestigious and unusual for the tiny portion of the French Syrah allowed in the blend. Lighter Chianti-style wines are made from Sangiovese blends, which includes one beloved native variety, Chiesa – a Lucchese Cynthiana.

Unlike modern American farmers, the farmers there, I noticed, generally practiced polyculture: grapes, olives for oil, usually some other fruit, and often cereal grains for livestock. Some sold fruit, herbs, olive oil – and such other goods as rabbits and shearling skins – while most of the grapes were shipped to the local wine cooperative. This is the situation in most of Europe's countless small wine regions where, as the masterful Australian wine writer James Halliday has observed, the wines rarely travel even thirty miles from home. There were a few owners who made and bottled wines at their own properties, but most people just let the co-op make the wine.

Our excellent day trips always ended back in Lucca, sometimes for satisfying and simple dinners at a restaurant owned by a friend of Nadine's and other times in the kitchen of our villa.

One day we drove three hours to Siena, an ancient walled city, and spent siesta watching the path of geometrical shadows in the bricked town centre, where an annual horse race between competitive families and clans attracts all of Europe.

We then drove an hour off the main highway to the medieval walled hamlet-winery of Castello di Volpaia, in the Chianti Classico appellation, and shouted and shouted and raised nobody. Finally, Nadine deciphered an envelope-sized note on the oak cellar door that said everyone was on holiday.

That afternoon, after Siena, we ended up in Montalcino, home of the red Brunello di Montalcino wines. The grapes, also called Brunello, a special clone of Sangiovese said to have been preferred through many centuries by the village's growers, are raised on all four faces of the 2,000-foot hill that juts up from the Tuscan plain. From the approach below, we cocked our heads at increasingly painful angles to see the village of Montalcino grow larger and larger in a fuzzy, warm dusk.

Along the rounded edges of the town, we stopped in our walk and looked out on the coming evening. There was no clear line where the broad flat plain and the fuzzy sky met. There was little wind or noise, and the sun sank in a wall of dust and smoke from fires of vine prunings which refracted a silent, soft magenta wash over everything. As was often the case on our trip, we found ourselves in a town of a few thousand people in an industrialized country at 6 p.m. – and ages away from the rest of the world.

The fellow at the wine store in Montalcino's 600-year-old fort told us in a poetic English/Italian patois how much pride local winegrowers took in their vineyards' distinct exposures.

"Those who face to the heated afternoon make a strong, hot wine which lasts many years," he slowly explained, "while those men to the eastern exposures" – he gestured skyward in countenance, pulling the words down from the heavens – "these wines come of the morning sun – very playful. These wines have, as well, a most exquisite perfume."

His demeanor switched to stiff and indifferent in describing Brunello from north-facing slopes, which may brood for twenty years before coming to life in bottle; southern-slope wines are known as likable and extroverted.

"You should select wines today of the 1988 vintage from either the east or the southern face of our hillside," he offered, leading me briskly then to a daunting row of Brunello dating back to the mid-1980s – perhaps fifty different labels from this tiny appellation – glowing under track lighting in a chestnut rack along an ancient wall of maroon brick.

"Let me help you," he said, as I fumbled with millions of lira.

So, clever as ever, I whipped out one of only five or six words I found could be understood in nearly every nation: "VISA?"

We drove back to Lucca, where a young chicken stuffed with lemon and herbs and baked in its clear sweet juices, Tuscan-style in a clay pot with small red potatoes, garlic, olive oil and rosemary, surely was not exceeded that night in any oven around us.

We stayed up late drinking two of the wines from our trip south. The 1990 Tenuta La Poderina Rosso di Montalcino smelled like raspberry jam smeared on hot rocks, its flavors seemingly wrung straight from the terrain, with tantalizing hints of dusty dry bushes and mineral pebbles. The 1990

Vineyard landscape near Lucca, Tuscany, 1994.

Nadine, River Arno, Florence, 1994.

Sangiovese from Paradiso, a small boutique producer in San Gimignano, had lush flavors but less definition, less breed and balance, and a tolerable hint of raisiny cough syrup on the nose. It reminded me of Zinfandel from Amador County, California, though brighter in fruit flavor.

I am a big believer in the importance of setting in drinking wine. For instance, as much as I love being outside and ringed around a fire, I find that wide open spaces don't favor good red wines so well. It seems they require a dining room to contain their aromas and charms. Sounds crazy, I know, but I've demonstrated it to my satisfaction many times.

It's one thing also to detect differences between a wine drunk with bread, olives, and cured sausage in yard chairs and the same wine with venison roast engulfed in warm dining room light on a snowy winter night. But I was not prepared at all for how different Italian wines tasted on home ground. They had such rapturous smells, while being rather austere in taste.

Traditional Tuscan grape varieties are prized for maintaining good acid balance in the warm summers, which helps explains how lighter, claret-type wines are rendered instead of the exuberant chunky reds typical of similarly hot California, where acid additions are often necessary during vinification. Whereas California's most acclaimed fine reds come from a variety (Cabernet Sauvignon) better suited, many traditionalists' insist, to cooler regions, Italy's Sangiovese is only now being planted to any great extent by California's wineries.

I confined myself in Italy to drinking almost exclusively Sangiovese-based wines, to narrow the gigantic fields that greets one in the wine stores. A favorite was the 1988 Chianti Classico Castello di Volpaia – I'd hoped to meet the makers on our trip there – with berry flavors so concentrated that they were like berry pastry filling; in structure, the wine had the exactness and refinement of great Bordeaux – at one-sixth the price.

Nadine said the Tuscan wines tasted the way the men had danced at Lucca's disco in the early '80s: with soul but not much shake.

It was no easy matter to tear ourselves away from Italy, and we made perfunctory pilgrimages to the realtor's office about a certain estate for sale pretty cheap in the high hills behind Lucca. "We'll get the legal work done while we're here," we announced, arm and arm on the way to dinner our final night, "and then all we've got to do when we get back is move our stuff over."

A thin, fire-cooked classic Tuscan rib steak with a lemon squeeze fired across it and the cafe's espresso brought us to our senses, though. Early the next afternoon, we were headed north along the sea, back toward Paris.

And through Provence. In Frejus, a dusty port town where those who can't afford St. Tropez moor their boats, I wanted to search out a domaine whose herb-laden red wine I had read about. The owner of a restaurant whose name translates to "Garlic Head" recommended his marvelously light and tangy house wine.

"Where is it made?" I asked him after dinner.

"Here in Frejus," replied Pierre Rais, eyes fluttering with mock surprise. "By Monsieur Jean Paquette," he added triumphantly. He gave us directions to Domaine de Curebeasse – the estate I had read about.

M. JEAN PAQUETTE does not sell his wine in America. He told us when we met the next day that he cannot find an importer to treat him fairly. He blends Cabernet Sauvignon deftly with Syrah, and the wine's firm currant-like, Bordeaux-like fruit is overlaid with pulled-back fragrances of orange peel, flowers and Provençal *garrigue* and herbs.

He was delighted when I produced a small bottle from my coat pocket, the '93 blend, with shocking levels of snappy cranberry fruitiness. When Cynthiana is young, no wine I've tasted from anywhere in the world exceeds its fruitiness; it's an absolute fruit bomb at six months old.

Jean Paquette smelled it, quickly tasted it, and arched his eyebrows. I thought the arching was a positive sign. He began chattering, looking at the glass as he carried it in the air. He moved steadily past us, dipping his head in acknowledgement, and into the next room, where we heard him say something; a sip; a pause; and a woman's voice break the brief silence.

Nadine and I looked at each other. "They're saying something about a flower," she said. I know next to no French. I gesture, point, and "I'm sorry" and "VISA" my way across international landscapes.

Presently, the Paquettes returned, talking excitedly in French, him with the glass in one hand, her holding a thick box the dimensions of a Scrabble game.

She sat the box on the counter, and he spoke in English. "This wine has a most incredible smell. I was telling my wife that it smells exactly like a certain flower we have here in Provence."

His box contained extracts and essences. Jean Paquette quickly went through the section on flowers, opening the tiny vials, sniffing, exclaiming. His wife was there, too, just as excited, reaching over his arms, sniffing, capping, opening, sniffing. All the while they spoke in fast, informal French. After two or three minutes, we could see they were not finding the flower they sought.

"Oh, oh," said Jean Paquette, intent but growing discouraged.

Through Nadine, I managed to explain that a typical aroma in young Cynthiana is coffee, or even cinnamon.

He understood both, but smelled neither. "It smells like gingerbread mostly to me when it's young," I told him.

He laughed and put his nose back over my wine. "I like it very much," he said. "Can you send me a bottle please, for my son to smell. I want my son to smell the wine. It is . . ." – he looked at his wife for words, and she too swirled the wine around. *"Très special,"* she breathed, without looking up.

"Oui, oui," said Jean Paquette, a glint in his eye. *"Très special.* I do not know how this flower, which only we have in Provence, got into your wine, Mr. Roberts!"

That night, back at the Garlic Head, we told Pierre Rais about our visit and enjoyed another of his fine, simply prepared meals. His chef cooks while Rais serves the local specialties in a quaint eatery of the sort that is still common in France and Italy, and all but absent in America. After dinner, I produced another of my trusty half-bottles, and made a very big deal about serving him and the half-dozen other guests in the bistro a splash of wine.

M. Rais also considered it "very special," before adding: "It's a bit thick, I would say."

So much for my drive for delicacy.

It would be absurd not to describe our visit to the famed Domaine Tempier in Bandol, a three hour drive from Frejus, west of Marseilles. I had read so much about the estate's wines, and the family's legendary hospitality toward Americans.

Upon tasting their 1987 in Pittsburgh, I had been struck by how similar it was in weight and structure to my Cynthiana. It even had some of Cynthiana's coffee and cinnamon on the nose.

That had been enough for me to write owner Lucien Peyraud, who had replied that his son and his son's wife, who spoke English, would be glad to see us. Lucien Peyraud is one of the great figures of French enology. He almost single-handedly rebuilt the reputation of Bandol by insisting that Mourvèdre was the grape which had, a century ago, given Bandol its distinctive personality and that, therefore, modern appellation regulations should require Mourvèdre to be at least 50 percent of the blend. Kermit Lynch, the California wine merchant who maintains a home nearby, tells Peyraud and Tempier's story so wonderfully that I refer anyone interested to his *Adventures on the Wine Route.*

Driving past the twisted trunks of Tempier's lower vineyard that afternoon, we passed a very old man ambling slowly along the road toward the domaine. Later, as Jean-Marie the winemaker son and wife Catherine were leading us to the cellar, the same senior was seating himself in a sunny, glassed-in room opening onto the vineyard. A ray of sun struck half across his body as he positioned himself in the chair, hands in front atop his planted cane.

"Who is that?" I said to Mme. Peyraud. She gave her husband a quick look, snickered, and said, "That is Jean-Marie's father, Lucien – Lucien Peyraud, to whom you wrote."

Well, nothing tastes like Bandol. Nothing tastes like Tempier, for that matter. Nadine and I were treated to barrel and bottle samples of the blackest, most tannic, most explosive red wines in my experience. I thought California had invented this style of winemaking. I was stunned.

Awkwardness set in when, in opening my own wine, its used cork was revealed. Jean-Marie was aghast when he saw the bright red wine stain on top, revealing that in an earlier incarnation the cork had faced the other way.

"I recycle corks," I said. I didn't tell him that if the cork leaks, I replace it with a better one. But I'm sure he would have known this, and I'm sure, in light of what happened next, that it wouldn't have mattered.

When my wine was poured, even I could tell a French wince. Mine are rustic and tender wines – who could not like their obvious fruity charms? – but they're not fancy, especially when young, and this one seemed anemic in color – a touch darker than Tempier's admired rosé.

The florid aromas of my Cynthiana wine bounced off the cave's treasured walls. Catherine and Jean-Marie sniffed at the rims of their glasses. They glanced at each other. They tasted.

He said something in French to her, then she turned her face just the slightest to address me. "Mr. Roberts," Catherine said evenly, "is this the wine that you wrote to say has something in common with the wine of the domaine?"

"They don't much resemble each other today, do they?" I replied in my best Ozarker yockel accent, all smiles, thinking this was not unlike a Monty Python routine. "What a wonderful wine you make here" is, I believe, what I croaked next.

Catherine translated, and Jean-Marie smiled pleasantly anyway. They were so nice. Really, they were.

I was simply too embarrassed to say that I had tasted only one vintage of Tempier – and it wasn't one of the domaine's famous wines from an individual vineyard. I had counted myself lucky to find even one regular vintage bottling in Pennsylvania, where the state runs the liquor business and the mediocrity of the selection is surpassed only by the outlandish prices.

The '87 was not a great year in Bandol – producing probably the lightest wine in two decades at Tempier. I didn't know that when I tasted it. And why hunt up another of their wines, I had reasoned after writing and receiving Lucien Peyraud's speedy reply, when I was going to taste them anyway at the source?

Nonetheless, it seemed that the Peyrauds liked my wine. Again, both described it as *"très special."*

The real achievement for an amateur, however, came when we returned to the sales room and Lucien Peyraud came in. I introduced myself, and Catherine told him that I was the American who had come to compare wines. He asked for a glass, and I poured from my bottle. He said, through Catherine, that he had heard many years ago of a grape with a name like Cynthiana being grown in the Midi, but he had never tasted the wine. Through Catherine, he also explained why the French, during the last twenty years, had pulled out nearly all hybrid varieties of American parentage (the French-American hybrids). "There was great excitement at one time, early in the century, but their wines were found to be inferior. Some people in France," he added, "believe the alcohol produced by the fermentation of such grapes to be poisonous."

He thanked me for pouring. He swirled it under his nose and into his mouth, and said something to Catherine which Nadine later noted contained the word "potable." ("My god, did you hear him?" I joked for months. "He said my wine was drinkable.")

"Monsieur Peyraud said your wine is good," translated Catherine.

The next afternoon, a Thursday, the Mediterranean at Cassis was warm to our toes, and a scruffy beach of cigarette butts and poodles being walked was pleasant enough to stretch out on in shirt-sleeves. The Cynthiana never tasted better than it did looking at the sun high over the sea with a tomato-caramelized onion-caper lunch pastry. By afternoon's end, Nadine's angular cheeks showed a sliver of sunburn from watching the winter throngs on the main boulevard beside the bay.

Back in Paris on the weekend, we ate dinner with some people Nadine knew – an American woman and her French postal worker husband. They asked us about Provence. We were curious, we explained: "What does it mean when someone says something is *très special?*" We told the Frenchman how everyone kept saying it after tasting my wine. "We know the literal translation, but what does it really mean?"

He let out a good laugh. Then, with his wife's help in English, he tried to explain the connotation.

"Is it a compliment?" I insisted.

He said it depends.

The phrase is, it seems, the English equivalent of "That's different," or "Interesting." He asked: "Do you know always times if someone likes when they say these words in English, too? It depends is the person open to a new experience, yes?

"It is the same in France, you see."

WINE-TRIPPING ACROSS France and Italy, Germany and Spain, and Bulgaria and Greece, too, should be required service for Americans interested in wine, and there is a certain tradition of it already.

Philip Wagner introduced French hybrid grapes to North America in the late 1930s after discovering them while traveling in France. Josh Jensen, owner of Calera Winery in California, is obsessed with Pinot Noir, and he concluded after many trips to Burgundy that the secret of its great wines were limestone soils (which he then sought out on a California mountain-top). Randall Graham, the mastermind of California's Bonny Doon Winery, best known for introducing Rhone-like reds to the state's winemaking corps, told me once that what he really enjoys is making brandy from unusual grapes that he found while trudging around Italy. Among them was the native American grape Noah. "A lot of those old Italian peasants have a little plot of Noah, and they use it for their best *grappa*," Graham says. "They only pull out that stuff once they decide you're 'okay.'"

Californian and Australian wineries receive high marks today for great technological contributions to the field, allowing ever larger quantities of wine to be made in factory settings, with factory-like pressures on the environment, too. But the Old World has lessons to teach that most New World winemakers have skipped over in pursuit of bigger, faster equipment and higher returns on investment.

There are two aspects of winemaking where this is particularly true. One is blending and the other is the use of oak, and I want to detour there for a moment because why it matters was disrobed for me only by my trip to Europe.

Of the 250 wines or so in my cellar today, probably two-thirds are blended reds from the southern France and northern Italy. While wines in this group can be rich and plump, more often they are restrained and medium-bodied. Generalizations are hard, but the most satisfying wines share a pure fruit flavor, and flower, herb, and mineral scents. In a proportion almost exactly opposite that of American wine, an overly oaked example is rare. This is probably because old, large upright oak vessels are still the preferred storage units in much of France and Italy – at Tempier, Jean-Marie Peyraud described with child-like tenderness the tedium of crawling inside his beloved tall, upright *foudres* and scrubbing their staves – whereas most U.S. wineries that use oak go for the 55-gallon barrels which impart a more aggressive woodiness to the wine.

American-style wine appreciation glorifies the oak barrel for use on near-ly all red wines, without comprehending what even French and Italian peas-ant-vintners know: very few grape varieties are capable of wines with such richness that they can stand up to the wood flavors small barrels impart.

Fine wine is "seasoned" with oak and, as with cooking, if a particular spice is distinctly noticeable in most recipes, the chef went overboard with it. Take the reds of France's Loire Valley, made primarily from Cabernet Franc. They are as common as butter in Parisian bistros, and so, one rarely sees them for sale in America. I could not get enough of these imagination-capturing wines. Berry-pure and pound-simple, they sent me away aching for the next mid-day snack with which to enjoy their balance and mineral-dipped charms. In all of vinous America there is not one replica of such Loire reds from Cab Franc. (Nominees may be mailed to my publisher!)

But one loses count in a single flip through a wine periodical of the reviews praising the "big, big, spicy oak nose" of Oak Manor Winery's Oak-Cask Olde Oaken Reserve, almost always made from Franc's richer cousin, Sauvignon. When you taste twenty, thirty, a hundred wines in an afternoon tasting session, or fly around tasting wines for a living as many pros do, aggressively oaky smells stand out, not fine-grained textures or subtle aro-mas. From a winemaker's standpoint, oak will get your wine noticed in America, so, the thinking goes, why bother with the population who likes to smell fruit and what the land can give to the wine?

Yet, I will take a blood-oath right now that with most foods, dense and oaky wines bore. With less and less meat in the modern diet – olive oil and tomatoes would be the hardest food items to replace around our house – fruit-and-spice Italian and French wines (and even the occasional moderately oaked U.S. wine) work beautifully.

I recognize this is the realm of aesthetics, so absolutes don't apply, but the lesson of my particular European pilgrimage was to redouble my com-mitment to red dinner wines that have lightness and substance. The style I aim for is more country than kingly, more berryish than brawny, and proba-bly the best models are the *grand cru* village wines of Beaujolais from Gamay – but not the soda pop sort of *nouveau* – or regional blends from Italy.

A bland commercialization of this concept, the "American food wine," has appeared in recent years which is still often overly oaky, just lighter.

Many producers seem to not understand that the wine has to be more interesting for its lightness. Applied to Cynthiana, I return to my first Stone Hill Norton years ago, and the heady, tannic, wood-aged surplus of flavor and acid it displayed. I just cannot drink such wines without thinking there's a lot of wasted energy.

The very knowledgeable specialist Charles Edson puts it this way: "Cynthiana needs a blender." It doesn't have a heavy enough skeleton to support gigantic flavors, he reasons, while wise blending can bulk up its frame and lengthen its flavors.

Others such as Philip Wagner have offered that when pure, Cynthiana wines are packed with "color, bouquet, plenty of tannin and acidity" – Wagner writing way back in 1937 – but the wine's "defect, as a matter of fact, is that it is apt to have all of these characteristics in too much abundance;" in too much abundance for its frame, I think, is what he meant. Edson and Wagner are making similar points really.

This strikes me as the same criticism that the most traditional Bordelais would have of the Cabernet Sauvignon grape. (An old-time Bordeaux becomes a rarer and rarer breed, thanks to the influence of British and American oak-loving wine writers.) Even the Californians, who invented the labeling of wines by grape variety, have come around to the logic that one can have too much of a good thing; thus, the proliferation in very recent years of the so-called "meritage" Cabernet-based blends.

Eastern U.S. winemakers are a couple of decades behind the Californians, however. Almost always a proprietor will tout a wine from a single varietal as his flagship creation, as if there's something meritorious in keeping the wine "pure."

I'm not saying pure is never divine. Sometimes, from very old Cynthiana vines, one of those inky, oaky unblended Missouri examples can achieve a singular power and intensity that is not unlike great Syrah wines of the Cote Rôtie in the Rhone Valley or even Brunello, also especially memorable when the vines are old. But most people will prefer a generally softer wine, and excessive oak-aging piles on sweet-sour wood smells and stiff wood tannins that, to me, flatter neither Cynthiana's wild grapyness, nor its naturally acidic pucker.

The sad fact is that the vast majority of American practitioners know little about wines in other parts of the world from native grapes of strong personality. For an aged red wine in the East, the usual reference is what's known as "Bordeaux style," a term that makes me inch for the winery door as soon as it leaves the owner's lips. What Bordeaux-style means, once the legendary American powers of reductive thinking are brought to bear, is a wine of high extract and long sojourn in barrel. ("Rhone-style," another term so broad as to be meaningless, has gathered momentum among U.S. wine writers and winemakers to describe non-Bordeaux-style wines made from Grenache and other grapes of Mediterranean origin.)

The problem is that these terms in no way account for the importance of blending in the wines of either Bordeaux or the Rhone Valley. On the best estates, the purpose of blending is to avoid a complete reliance on one grape in the vineyard, which could be disastrous to a property in the event of a total failure of that variety in a given year. The practice has roots in social history in France; a harvest failure used to spell economic depravity. The same hedge, the logic of diversification, once drove winegrowers throughout most of France and Italy to mix in cereal grains and orchard fruits with wine grapes. One still sees it, but polyculture is definitely on the run. And not many wine lords in California, meanwhile, worry about being able to feed the cows or having some grain to mill for flour.

In the cellar, diversification allows the vintner to fill holes or tame the flavors of wine rendered from a principal variety. Of the eight most famous European red wine districts – Rioja (Spain); Dão (Portugal); Bordeaux, Midi, Rhone, Burgundy, Beaujolais (France); Chianti, Piedmont (Italy) – only three (Burgundy, Beaujolais, and Piedmont) attained world-wide fame with unblended wine. (Arguably, the Cote Rôtie's pure Syrahs could be broken out of the Rhone, as could Brunello of Italy, making two more unblended standouts, but I'd also say that clonal variation among the many different Pinot Noir vines grown in Burgundy, as is also true with the Gamay family in Beaujolais, nearly qualifies them as blended wines.) More importantly, in every case, the traditional wine from the full range of other grape varieties permitted by law in the blend (up to seventeen varieties, including whites, are allowed in the wine of Chateauneuf-du-Pape) is widely considered to be superior to a wine from the district made only from the dominant variety. In many famous districts, in fact, regulations do not permit pure varietals.

From Chianti Classico or Chianti Ruffina, for example, pure Sangiovese is available, but something is missing when Cananaiolo and Malvasia aren't included, and the wine sells for correspondingly less.

Take, as another example, the Grenache grape. Chateau Rayas in France makes a tremendous 100 percent cuvee from this variety, but otherwise Grenache is a significant base wine for blending in three Mediterranean wine districts (and in California, as well).

To bring this discussion home, Grenache possesses a shortcoming oddly opposite of Cynthiana's: the best wines from Grenache are wise graftings of more pungent flavors, aromas, and textures onto its fruity but fairly neutral frame. And really, the same must be said of Sangiovese, the Midi's Carignan, and Rioja's Tempranillo.

BLENDING HAS A LONG TRADITION, and I reasoned there had to be something to it. Among wines I adored, I certainly felt I could taste the difference.

The 1983 Chateau Potensac, a *Cru Bourgeois* from the central Medoc of Bordeaux, drunk on its tenth birthday, was among the top three or four best integrated wines I've had: nutmeg and leather on the nose, and then graceful velvet berries – no particular berry flavor – that were subdued but very exciting. It went right to the edge of not enough oak, but ended dignified – country-generous, instead of blaring out with wood flavors.

California's 1988 Bellerose Reserve Cabernet, at six years old, had a restrained spicy bouquet and the same super-fine tannins wrapping complex fruit, though it was more classically blackberry and cassis than Potensac. The striking feature of the Bellerose, from Sonoma County, was also its sense of integration; nothing poked out, no oaky flashes. If I'd been near a phone, instead of beside a campfire when I drank it – in violation of my rule about fine red wine drunk outdoors; but hey, it was trout season – I would have called winemaker Charlie Richard and piled on the praise. The 1988 California red vintage is thought of as weak, but he had told me when I visited him in 1993 that he considered it a great year and the best Cabernet he'd ever made.

Richard was making "meritage" wines well before they were fashionable in his state, having opened his winery in the early 1980s. So was Guenoc Winery in Lake County, starting in 1980, the bottling which provoked my first personal wine pilgrimage to California. (I rapped on the door at the winery on a day it was closed, begging – successfully – to be let in.) As at Potensac, these wineries blended the full contingent of Bordeaux varieties – the two Cabernets, Merlot, Malbec, and Petit Verdot – and Richard even grows them organically. The elegant firmness and the mineral traces of Geunoc's Lake County wines are highly distinctive.

Wholeness, not bigness, is the result as well in so-called "field blend" examples of California Zinfandel. When they established their vineyards two generations ago, early Italian growers liked to include Petite Syrah, Grenache, Barbera, Alicante Bouschet, and sometimes other varieties into the vineyard block, up to about twenty-five percent, and often with no systematic placement. Zinfandel tends to ripen unevenly, and to excess, and mixing in other varieties with more moderate alcohol potential was the grower's way of ensuring a balanced table wine. Without such varieties to temper the gleanings from these old parcels, monster Zinfandels are born; too often, they are block-headed wines, with alcohol levels of 15 percent or more. They are enjoying a revival right now, and they certainly constitute a regional specialty, but I often wonder how many of their proponents were around twenty-five years ago during the last California fascination with such tyrants. I can never figure out what to serve with a Zinfandel the color of tar and nearly as thick, though I don't know why I worry since few dinner guests notice after two fill-ups of wine only a couple of degrees shy of port. California's last tryst with that style of Zinfandel ended with a polar swing all the way to White Zinfandel, which, ironically, saved the variety from being grubbed out in many areas of California during the 1980s. Only in the last decade has the variety rebounded as a red wine grape.

By contrast, "field-blending" can produce understated treasures – to me, the most exciting style of wine – which combine gracefulness and decadent density in one bottle.

Factoring such wines in with sublime blends from Chianti and the Rhone, I set out to compare winemaking practices among the regions in

Europe that rely on blending. Many producers use a fermentation method in closed vats called carbonic maceration, or at least a high percentage of whole clusters fermented in open vats. The typical style is wine with essentially an acidic structure (as opposed to a tannic structure) that softens with age, and intense fruitiness from the whole cluster fermentation that gives the wine special tastiness when young. This is also what gives Beaujolais, many of those Loire reds, and Burgundy to a somewhat less extent such a nice young face.

Fermentation methods for red wines are, like all aspects of red winemaking, more complicated than for making whites. Having the skins involved presents options that are not there when mere juice is to be transformed.

Words of book instruction are useful as general guides, but they cannot be expected to instruct on such highly personal matters. My own notions continue to evolve, perhaps because the precise intersection of grace and force fluctuates. The considerations span the most fascinating parts of winemaking, and selecting from among the parts shows how aesthetic and artisanal impulses may be expressed in this liquid medium.

Typically, less skin contact is advised for making red wine more supple; more contact is suggested for age-worthy wines, the *vin de garde,* as the Bordelais say. Longer skin contact concentrates aromatics and flavors. While this is perhaps another way of saying a wine is "less supple," who could argue that most any wine is made better if the bouquet and flavors are more penetrating?

The real issue is that both good and bad elements are concentrated by longer skin contact, and here wine becomes a metaphor for a crucial concept that marks – if I may be so bold – human existence. Surprising? Why? We should not be surprised to find profundities in wine; we're often called upon to contemplate them in paintings in a museum or in tracing the rim of a bowl in a potter's studio.

Going one step farther, Paul Shepard, in *Nature and Madness*, points out that since the advent of agriculture, humans have tended to regard "wild things" as bad, since they are "enemies of the tame." (Scholarly linkages of this ethic to Christianity are also available, of course.) What is lost in keeping nature down is an appreciation, says Shepard, of a "complementary entity embracing friendly and dangerous parts in a unified cosmos. . . ." A forest without the wolf or cougar is permanently safe for humans, as far as predators go anyway, but are safety, convenience, and certainty of human dominion the highest values that our age can tolerate? By analogy: a swallow of red wine made with long skin contact will have a fleshy, inviting fruitiness often ending with a little bite of darkness, of mortality, of death – the mystical.

Skin contact concentrates both warm, friendly berry parts and acidic, aggressive ones. Skin contact complicates flavors, at once softening and enhancing them by making the "flavor chains longer," as I recall from Bo Barrett's tutelage at Montelena.

It is almost always true that wines made with long skin contact are more persistent and more flavorful, but determining the skin contact that each wine in each vintage can tolerate is a real trick.

There is no proper ratio of the opposing parts in winemaking; it must be discovered by every person. A third Paul – Paul Draper of California's Ridge Winery – has said that all winemakers who strive to make art in wine must decide the degree to which he or she is willing to allow the "chaos in."

ALMOST ALL commercial wineries today exclude the chaos: few consumers, after all, are prepared to contemplate metaphysical issues in a goblet of wine.

I use whole cluster fermentations, then extend the skin contact once the berries collapse and break up during fermentation. This is way different from the standard recipe in eastern America but quite logical when practices in other parts of the world are counted. This recipe is the traditional one in Spain's Rioja, for instance. Then I blend flavors from other grapes for nuance.

Although standardization seems to be advancing on many fronts, its opposite is also making inroads, it seems. For instance, Daniel Gehrs has turned out exciting craftwork at three different California wineries during the last decade, most recently at Zaca Mesa on the Central Coast. For three years, we treasured his butterscotch-pie of a Pinot Blanc (Congress Springs 1990, from an old block of the variety planted in Monterey County), and I still have a couple of bottles stashed away for the new century. He also bottles wines under his own label, and his Chenins age like the real article from the Loire, gaining a honeyed richness by Year 6 or 7 in good years. His 1991 Sonoma County Zinfandel sticks in my mind like a first kiss. Truly a successful "claret" from Zin, it glided across the tongue as raspberries and cream, with a little flaky pastry, too. There was also an absolute river of swirling soft fruit. I still get a little shaky thinking about how gorgeous that wine was.

In truth, Europe and not California leads the campaign away from factory wine. Distinct examples are made at the edge of Provence in the foothills of the Alps. I buy every one of the handcrafted vintages of Domaine de la Gautiere. The 1988 is rustic and true, a heady wine entirely different yet in no way superior to the much lighter wines the property turned out from 1990 to 1992 using mainly Grenache and Syrah.

The estate uses no chemical insecticides, herbicides, or fungicides to grow grapes, and the owners supplement the winery's cash-flow with their own honey, herbs, and flowers. The winery practices a sort of polyculture that many new thinkers in U.S. agriculture believe is the best path to success as a modern farmer.

I learned of Gautiere from Kermit Lynch's *Adventures on the Wine Route.* A U.S. importer of mainly petite French wines, many of them $7 vin de pays like Gautiere, Lynch is one American who does see the subject in a global context. He decries how America's preference for established varietals is leading to the homogenization of wine aesthetics. Similarly, Philip Wagner complained to me in a 1990 interview that "you'd think there are only two grapes left in the world – Cabernet and Chardonnay."

Lynch also is no spokesman for Cabernet Sauvignon. "It has always seemed too easy, almost monotonous," he writes, because it makes a "decent wine everywhere it ripens." Cabernet's flavor "tends to dominate environmental factors, unlike the Pinot Noir, Syrah, or Mourvèdre, for example, which express environmental factors." Unfurling a scholarly list of examples – the hawthorn blossom in young Hermitage, wild cherries or leathery esters in various Burgundies – Lynch then asks the seemingly innocent question: "Is the Gautiere *vin de pays* better than Chambertin? The Gautiere is delicious and it has soul . . . but what a question: Is it better than Chambertin? 'Better for what?' is the only proper reply.

"Better when dining at Taillevent, the Parisian gastronomic palace. No, at Taillevent, the noblest bottles are appropriate."

Is it better than "Chambertin served alongside black olives and sliced sausage? Yes.

"With ratatouille? Yes.

"Hot onion omelet with vinegar sauce? Yes."

With a steamy bowl of homemade soup? You bet, Lynch would say.

Great wine has its place, as he insists, and we should cherish those places. But for most occasions, we should expect something more humble and count ourselves lucky if it is made by people intent on expressing their particular union with a piece of land in a particular year. Such wines will do just fine.

CALIFORNIA AUTHOR David Darlington, who in 1991 wrote *Angels' Visits: An Inquiry into the Mysteries of Zinfandel,* is among the new wave of writers leading the publishers of wine books into lands beyond the safe and classic haunts of Bordeaux, Burgundy, and Germany, or Napa and Sonoma valleys in California.

The book's title comes from an 1888 comment by a legendary California winegrower named George Husmann. Husmann wrote that he had "yet to see" the red wine he preferred "to the best samples of Zinfandel produced in this state. Unfortunately these best samples are like angels' visits, 'few and far between.'"

Before arriving in California, during a less well-known chapter in his career, Husmann had helped build Missouri's wine industry into the nation's second largest. In 1865, he had felt that one Missouri wine "had not its equal among all the foreign red wines."

That wine was made from Cynthiana.

Husmann fashioned a publishing career about winegrowing that began in 1859 and ended twenty-eight years later in California. In addition to writing four books, he delivered presentations at numerous agricultural fairs and penned dozens of articles in the popular press and journals, including one he edited from 1869 to 1872. He was a tireless promoter of Norton and Cynthiana, which he said was different from Norton. Husmann, incidentally, claims to have introduced Cynthiana to Missouri, in 1858, from cuttings obtained from the Prince nursery on Long Island.

Husmann's numerous winegrowing enterprises involving Cynthiana ended, variously, with the sacking of his winery near Hermann by Confederate troops to outright bankruptcy to what apparently was financial salvation as a nurseryman. He is best known in the history of winegrowing as one of the four principal suppliers of native American rootstocks and their hybrids to European growers after the outbreak of phylloxera on the continent in the 1870s. (Reams of literature chronicle the importation of the tiny root-eating louse to Europe on American vines. The pest, which did not prey on American vines, then spread throughout Europe's vineyards and began eating *vinifera* roots, which are fatter than U.S. vine roots. *Vinifera* quickly succumb to the bug's ravages.)

More importantly, however, than Husmann's considerable personal fame were those with whom Husmann was well acquainted in Missouri. This group of progressive-minded German immigrants and sons of immigrants around St. Louis were intent upon turning the Missouri and Mississippi river valleys into a New World Rhineland. They made the Midwest's wine history.

Their activities, which ranged far beyond the state's borders, deserve special scrutiny because they neatly highlight wine's important though largely ignored position in human migration, social history, and culture, and because such focus will advance the story of Cynthiana considerably. No other group did more to bring recognition to the variety's wines.

To begin the account, Husmann's own words are appropriate. The year is 1850, the setting is Hermann, 50 miles along the high bluffs of the Missouri River from St. Louis, and "the attention of some of our grape-growers was drawn towards a small, insignificant looking grape, which had been obtained by a Mr. Wiedersprecker from Hr. Heinrichs, who had brought it from Cincinnati, and, almost at the same time, by Dr. Kehr, who had brought it with him from Virginia." The Missouri growers discovered in the next two years that the Norton vine "kept its foliage bright and green," and that its fruit was not damaged, though fungus diseases routed the in-vogue variety, Catawba.

Cincinnatian Nicolas Longworth, the Robert Mondavi of the U.S. wine trade from roughly 1835 to 1850, had experimented with Norton in the Ohio River Valley and pronounced it "worthless." As I noted earlier, the species does not root readily from cuttings, so expanding its acreage cheaply and quickly was not easy – a definite drawback to rapid empire-building. Still, Husmann observes, "we thought Mr. Longworth was human and might be mistaken, and trusted as much to the evidence of our senses as to his verdict."

The hills around Hermann afford long, scenic views of the surrounding countryside and of the great river that linked these German pioneers to their dynamic new world; candor is exceeded in their writings only by an uncommon open-mindedness.

"Wine was made from it in larger quantities," Husmann continues, "and now that despised and condemned grape is the great variety for red wine. . . ." By 1865, he says, he had visited Ohio, and true enough, "it does not look there as if it were the same grape. And why should it? They drove it from them and discarded it in its youth; we fostered it, and do you not think, dear reader, there sometimes is gratitude in plants as well as men?"

Husmann's father had been a member of the Philadelphia Settlement Society, which founded Hermann in 1837 after an idealized, romantic, and very effective report on the land thereabouts by one Gottfriend Duden. The report was published in Germany in 1829. Duden sought to spark immigration to the area where he'd already bought a farm. Realizing the importance of viniculture "for immigrants from the Rhineland," Duden insisted they would find "a ready market and high prices, for the Americans look upon viniculture as a national matter, saying the Old World has nothing to offer them except wine."

Duden's report was one among many idealized accounts of New World conditions. Large-scale migration to the country was in full swing; many German republics convulsed with civil strife. Once those wanderers convinced by Duden arrived in Missouri, they found a thin, rocky soil along with the promised pastoral charms. These immigrants were unique in that a considerable number of the men had some university training. Deploying skills learned from their fathers and grandfathers in stony regions of Germany and Switzerland, several turned to viniculture. By the end of the Civil War, Hermann had about 1,000 acres of vines; towns such as Dutzow, Freeburg, and Washington had considerable wine-related commerce; a nearby hill town, Augusta, with several hundred acres of vines, was a virtual monoculture town, its historic counterparts being wine cantons in the Rhine or Rhone river valleys.

Indeed, when the U.S. government began in 1980 to approve more specialized regional appellations for wine production, Augusta, with its long winegrowing heritage and distinctive balance of favorable climate and soil, was the first new appellation approved.

With Hermann at its western extreme, the German population of eastern Missouri could claim by the middle of the nineteenth century as prominent a position in a region's cultural and political life as any immigrant group anywhere in America. Intent upon maintaining key facets of their German heritage – they possessed "networking" skills to make a 1990s' marketing team envious – the Missouri Germans built a reputation for excellence in science and commerce that endures to this day.

In addition to George Husmann, there was Friedrich Muench (state senator, political essayist and winegrower); Jacob Fugger (first to plant grapes at Hermann); Michael Poeschel (first winemaker); Jacob Rommel (first to make a Norton wine and later a grape hybridizer of international status); Dr. George Engelmann (a St. Louis physician and world famous botanist). There were literally dozens of others. The collected vinicultural talent and the "quantity of technical writing" about the subject probably could not be equaled anywhere in the world at the time, notes Thomas Pinney in his scholarly *A History of Wine in America.*

There were a half-dozen German-language newspapers in St. Louis by the 1850s, and most served a large regional audience among the German, Swiss, and Alsatian populations within a 100-mile radius of the city. Rising to prominence in the crucible of Civil War-era tensions, both capitalizing on and guiding calls for a truly egalitarian society of newcomers – the great promise of the Prairie and western states – these papers were among the first powerful lobbies for a leader who would confront local antagonists, the southern plantation owners, and the eastern Anglo-Saxon establishment which were all equally wicked in the eyes of midwestern German editorialists.

It is no coincidence that Abe Lincoln rose from the prairie grass of central Illinois rather than the New York bowery.

"No German in Missouri has ever led a Negro astray. . . . There is no state law the Germans have ever violated in a treasonous manner," wrote Muench in 1860, in response to state legislation proposed by those he called "haters of liberty." The personal papers of this incredible man, known as "old Father Muench" by close friends, wound up in the Harvard University Archives.

"Drive us out and ruin us then," Muench thundered rhetorically at the Old Guard, "since you can no more rob us of our sensibilities and convictions than you can take away our right to vote, our freedom of expression, and our free press. Stop being an American and become an Austrian or a Neapolitan. . . ."

A VIBRANT WINE industry in Missouri was part of the Germans' plan to capitalize on their own traditions while civilizing the attitudes surrounding them. The individual model was the yeoman farmer, whose impending loss Thomas Jefferson had decried a generation earlier. But the Missouri German yeomen "were not tenant farmers but independent proprietors, prepared to take an experimental and scientific interest in viticulture," as Pinney describes them in his excellent general history of U.S. wines (to which I am greatly indebted here).

Muench summarized the plan in 1859, writing: "If the Germans here are to accomplish anything at all beyond improving agriculture, horticulture and viticulture, or of lifting the level of several crafts, then they will have to preserve their language and education against the onslaught" of American culture and education.

So insistent were these immigrants on education as the fount of both financial and social empowerment that they earned the label locally of *Lateinische bauern* – "Latin peasants," or farmers who could not only read, but who could read Latin. German, by the way, was the first language in some central Missouri school districts well into the twentieth century.

Muench had schooled at Giessen University as a Lutheran minister, was a prominent political essayist for 40 years, and managed to issue two books on viniculture; he devoted his life to the culture of the grape in the grandest sense, growing Cynthiana for his Augusta winery (now Mount Pleasant Winery). Pinney observes that "something of Muench's high-minded style may be had from this passage in his *School for American Grape Culture:* 'The vine-dresser, free, lord of his own possessions, in daily intercourse with peaceful nature, is a happier and more contented man than thousands of

Missouri wineland countryside, early morning.

Heinrich Grohe, 1998. *Photograph by John Trotter.*

those who, in our large cities, driven about by the thronging crowd, rarely attain true peace and serenity of mind.'" When Muench died in 1881, it happened, according to Husmann, "among his beloved vines, one fine winter's morning . . . with the pruning shears still in his hand, in his 84th year."

Within a decade, the Missouri industry was in serious decline. By the time Prohibition came, there was little wine left to outlaw in the state, and not until the 1960s did commercial winemaking rebound in Missouri.

Much of the spirit of the region's settlers lingers today. A visit to its hills and valleys dotted with tidy farms, modern and successful wineries, and fine home-cooking restaurants – my wife and I have a favorite in Washington, Cowan's, that has no earthly peer for quality of preparation at reasonable prices – is like a whap in the face for anyone thinking "old European traditions" haven't persisted in our country's interior.

One must go 40 miles south, though, to the northernmost plateau of the Ozarks, to find a surviving example of the traditional nineteenth century "independent proprietor" and craftsman vintner. His winery is the antithesis of today's corporate wine factory, as he is the antithesis of the dashing, college-trained winemaker working for a millionaire owner dabbling in wine.

The white wines of Heinrich Grohe, an engineer by training and a German by birth, are politely fruity, somewhat steely, and at times very subtle – as nervy as Heinrich himself. The red Baco Noir wine that Grohe made in 1983 was a demure, pale ruby beauty of strawberry-tasting fruit and graceful lightness. It spurred my interest in tantalizing and delicate red wines. It still affects how I make my reds.

Grohe also fashions a Cynthiana, which he ferments at temperatures cooler than most would endorse, to render a wine of special fragrance, redolent of summer flowers and herbs, but also coffee, bacon, and leather. He believes passionately in pure varietal wines and perhaps for this reason does not think much of my Cynthiana interpretations. So, instead, I take him barrel-fermented Vidal or Vignoles, or dry blueberry, and he'll ante up with an experiment of his own. I never fail to visit Heinrichshaus Vineyard & Winery on trips to Missouri, and my heart skips every time I encounter Heinrich, in burgundy beret and usually overalls, with a fire burning in his rustic tasting room near St. James. Nadine and I both cherish the hour we spend beside his stove every year.

Pinney, a definite authority on German winemakers, told me when we spoke in 1992 that he was planning a book on their importance in American wine. Husmann, he observes in his book, is "symbolic of the fortunes of winegrowing in the United States itself, for it touched many points of development and mirrored many representative changes."

In 1881, "as though to symbolize the transference of power from the East to the West" in America, Husmann moved to California to save a 300-acre wine estate from phylloxera, which had eaten its way across the state's *vinifera*-studded landscape. Knowledge gained in Missouri on the subject opened Husmann's second career in California, and he was busy throughout the 1890s writing books and selling technical advice.

Pinney adds that "there was nothing meretricious, nothing affected" in Husmann's actions. He was simply a "true believer."

THE DEAR READER may be forgiven for wondering why, if these Latin farmers were so accomplished, isn't Hermann a world-famous wine district and why isn't Cynthiana wine served at state dinners in the nation's capital?

I wondered for the better part of two decades. A lot of different theories are advanced. Robert Scheef says Prohibition doomed the industry. But the number of wineries in the state was declining years before the Drys took the pulpit. Such explanations describe symptoms rather than causes.

So, I was happy to make the acquaintance of Peter Poletti. An assistant professor at the University of Missouri-St. Louis, Poletti did his doctoral dissertation in American Studies on the Missouri wine industry. Poletti knows a lot about the larger historical currents that affected the industry.

"Why did it collapse? Really it collapsed for two reasons," he said in a 1994 interview. "First, the railroad, once it came through, brought juice and wine by the tanker load of more consistent quality than could be produced by Missouri winegrowers, or winegrowers anywhere else, for that matter.

"This was the mindset then. The country was expanding rapidly, mass markets were growing, and producers felt they had to produce for the mass market or they wouldn't survive.

"Secondly, there were so many jobs in the cities, and by comparison to jobs on the farm, they were high-paying." The cities were exploding. St. Louis, for instance, doubled its population in the twenty-five years at the end of the 1800s. "Once the kids heard about these jobs, and there's no way they couldn't," says Poletti, "they wouldn't stay on the farm. It's the classic story of opportunities in the city draining all the workers away from the country."

"The only ones left were the ones who couldn't afford to leave," I said, having caught on, "and the few craftsmen among the winegrowers."

"Exactly," answered Poletti, "and this was a tiny percentage by, say, 1900, and in the end even they couldn't stand up to what the railroad brought because the railroad also totally changed buying habits. People cared much less about buying locally."

"It's the Wal-Mart mentality," I said. "Buy it cheaper, don't matter where it comes from. Don't matter if it puts all my neighbors out of business. So, you don't think it was black rot and mildew diseases," (reasons typically cited) "or growing Prohibitionism?"

"Those were minor compared to the railroad and destruction of the farm economy." Poletti gave a sad sigh. "The point is who is going to be a farmer under those conditions?"

I am struck by how the story of the German vinicultural paradise ended. It fits neatly into historical currents of western settlement, and to come full circle, into how the countryside today seems to be filled by humans who have no zeal for making a living from what the land offers. So many simply hang on to the family's land. But a productive, thriving farm economy requires, after all, imaginative and spirited farmers first and foremost.

What happened to Missouri's wine industry seems such a pure example of what the late historian Christopher Lasch called "the increasing inequalities introduced by the market" in his scholarly examination of social mobility. What did the German essayist mean when he said the vine-dresser, a farmer, was "free, lord of all his possessions?" The definition of freedom is a whirlpool of subjectivity. But clearly, as Lasch would insist, these Latin farmers achieved the best form of social mobility, one defined as much by competence in their trades and active lives of the mind as by their incomes.

One visitor impressed by what he saw on the farms of the period was the Frenchman Michel Chevalier. He reflected that among American farmers, "the great spiritual traditions are harmoniously combined in his mind with the principles of modern science," while the rural peasantry in Chevalier's nation dwelt on "biblical parables" and "gross superstition."

Lasch adds that "restless" curiosity, a skeptical and iconoclastic turn of mind, and resourcefulness "dramatically seemed to differentiate" farm people and other laborers in America from their European counterparts.

Scholars will argue about the specialness of the era in which these German winegrowers excelled; life was fairly good for the skilled craftsmen whose work alone or in small shops dominated local and regional economies, but historians point out how far less pleasant life was for those trying to work their way into the system – those trying for a slice of the pie. The pall of slavery hung over the land. The Civil War divided families, turned neighbor against neighbor. And in the latter years of the era, technological change came at revolutionary speed.

Often when I see Heinrich Grohe, I want to broach the subject of Missouri's old-time German winegrowers, to see if he's aware of the tradition, to see if he feels any historical affinities. But, I'm gone from my native place, and well, I don't know him well.

So, instead, I shall use this space to rhapsodize for just a moment about being white, literate, and living in the countryside as an independent winegrower in middle America in the middle of the nineteenth century.

I can feel the sun on my cheeks. Time would have passed so fast had it been mine. . . .

But I rhapsodize about such things . . . just as Abraham Lincoln was known to do. The most enduring result of making a living from the land, Lincoln said, "is the effect of thorough cultivation upon the farmer's own mind."

DURING OUR VISIT in 1993 to Heinrich Grohe, I mentioned to him that Nadine and I had begun to look for property on which to build a winery. The words just sort of popped out. Maybe, I said, trying out the idea as much for ourselves as for Heinrich, we'd end up at Scenery Hill. Nadine and I had never discussed the idea in any detail, so I was surprised to see little surprise on her part. She simply smiled and said yeah, maybe.

~ SIX ~

"And all the flowers were dancing/
One by one they all told me about the time that had been/
and about all the time that will be." – Jimmie Dale Gilmore,
"Thinking of You"

NEW SEASON'S GROWTH from a bud on a branch of a grape plant
seems to me almost like magic, for I never paid much attention to such
small wonders until I started farming. The tiny bud is not unlike a jack-in-
the-box: within two weeks of its opening in spring, tiny fruit clusters emerge
clinging delicately to eager shoots that seem to lengthen before one's eyes.
Remarkably, the infant bunches come from sunray and carbohydrate energy
made the previous season and stored through the winter in the bud. Each
summer, starting in June, one can see the buds that will provide next season's
growth forming beside the current season's young leaves.

The fruit bunches in early spring are beautifully soft, fuzzy miniatures of
subtle vermilion, ochre, chartreuse, rust. As they grow, pin-head-sized
bumps within the cluster swell to reveal individual berry forms – potential
grapes. It is the pollination of these flowering forms, roughly six weeks after
bud-break, which makes a berry.

From one to four clusters of berries, two clusters being the norm, then
space out along the shoot, which hardens to greenish-brown by mid-season.
These branches, called "canes" once they turn brown and harden, will grow
on vigorous varieties such as Cynthiana to a length of 6 feet or more by season's end. On proper soil, with a proper amount of seasonal growth, canes of

3 to 4 feet are ideal.

For pollination of its flowers, grapevines do not rely on bees, as do fruit trees; instead, grapes are "self-pollinating," meaning wind does the bees' work of spreading pollen. Rain or high winds are feared at flowering because the flower's cap can be prematurely dislodged on some varieties, thus aborting pollination and causing the berry not to "set." Among the classic varieties, for example, Merlot is so prone to poor berry set that the June rains common in Bordeaux regularly have first dibs on the *grand cru* blend for that vintage. Nature always has a hand to play, and it's one reason the Bordelais diversify: less Merlot may force the vintner to use more Cabernet Sauvignon, Cabernet Franc, and often Petit Verdot and Malbec, but at least the vintage is not a total loss, as it would be if Merlot were relied on exclusively.

Merlot grown in areas with settled weather at flowering is among the more reliable producers, which partly explains its rising status worldwide.

But whether it be Merlot for Chateau Petrus or Concord for Welches, grape pollen on the wind during the early weeks of summer is one of nature's classiest perfumes. In grape districts, the distinctive fragrance can be almost overwhelming; even in the wooded countryside a pressing sweetness from the esters of flowering wild grapes hangs heavily in the air of an early summer evening.

ANXIETY RISES IN STILL AIR, however, for the grape grower. Summer dew and humidity are perfect media for the spread of fungal diseases – downy and powdery mildew, black rot, and phomopsis – throughout eastern America and much of Europe. Most of California, like the desert growing areas of other western states, faces much less disease pressure, as do the more arid wine districts of Europe; the most devastating of the fungal attackers, black rot, is nearly unheard of in dry climates.

In eastern America, practically all grape varieties are susceptible to the diseases, while a few varieties, such as Cynthiana, have natural resistance to black rot or some of the other ailments. Once ripening begins, in early August typically, black rot no longer attacks the fruit on most varieties, but an outbreak early in the season, shortly after berry set, allows the disease a long and disastrous run through June and July.

Chemical fungicides provide a protective coating on foliage and developing berries, and prevention is key because the disease cannot easily be eradicated once established. More and more chemicals are appearing on the market that work not as shields, but rather within the plant's vascular system. Although they generally are more effective, many people worry that these more invasive chemicals may also more easily end up in the wine.

Black rot reveals its presence with brown to black elliptical spots on the leaves and shoots. The blemishes virtually guarantee that the fruit will be affected within a few days. Persistent spraying at this point can restrain black rot's spread and damage, but the grower needs nature's cooperation, which is hard to obtain: rainstorms every few days, a predictable mid-summer pattern in continental climates, can wash away spray material as fast as it can be applied. Plus, dripping rain spreads the disease spores so that eventually the fungus gets the upper hand.

Entire crops can be lost to hideous brown craters which, in as little as 48 hours, engulf and shrivel the grape.

"I watched it eat my crop practically in front of my eyes," recalled a friend about the rainy, humid summer of 1992 in western Pennsylvania.

Ideas about protecting plants from disease overlap into areas that have nothing to do with growing plants, and, in my case, everything to do with long-range plans for making a living at farming. My focus of course is viticulture, but growers of corn, soybeans, and other row crops, as well as fruit and vegetable growers, all face analogous pressures from plant diseases.

In winegrowing, companies or individuals with large vineyards, with what are considered great sums of money at stake, express a mainly paranoid view of nature by applying fungicides every seven to fourteen days from early April through early August, with other applications spaced out in the weeks before harvest. The goal is to provide a constant chemical shield to disease.

But in many parts of the world and now increasingly in America, farmers are taking the initiative to reduce the presence of active chemicals in the living environment and chemical residue on crops, in soil, in underground aquifers, and in rivers, lakes, and ocean estuaries. Such a philosophy of farming, practiced in varying degrees and referred to by various names, may be broadly labeled as "sustainable farming." Practitioners in America are believed to number only a few thousand – less than 10 percent of all farmers – though some aspects of a sustainable farming regimen are in use on nearly every farm.

Growers who pursue sustainable viticulture seek to protect the vines only during especially critical periods and only when conditions are optimum for the spread of the very worst diseases. In a not-at-all figurative sense, the grower must come down from the mount – his usual position riding a tractor above the plants – and walk among them. This is required far more with a sustainable approach than in chemical-dependent farming.

Leaf and shoot surface tell all; the color of good and healthy life is bright green, but sickness is also part of life, so helping the plant to overcome its regular ailments primarily with its own energies builds the bond between us and plants just as shared adversity can tighten the bond between many mammals. It may sound strange – plants that can "feel" and "think" – but it's among the truths I can confirm by experience. With this approach, chemical applications are greatly reduced. Great attention is paid to weather conditions and patterns. If disease is not fully prevented, the goal becomes a less extensive outbreak, with less damage. Control is less "perfect." Balances are sought, losses are accepted.

Not every incidence of black rot, for example, leads to total destruction of the crop. Fewer spray applications, timed properly and adjusted to weather conditions, will delay the disease's onset so that ripening begins before catastrophic losses occur.

Wes Parker, director of the Land Institute in Kansas, defines sustainable farming as simply "good farming . . . practices that don't consume ecological capital or otherwise degrade the landscape." Most aboriginal agriculture in what is today North America was carried on using what would be considered sustainable techniques. Other cultures in other parts of the world have done it and are doing it.

A pure "organic farmer" is one who eschews all synthetic chemical sprays. In winegrowing, organic sprays from lime and copper rather than synthetic chemicals are the antiseptic agents for the plant surface. Several large quality-oriented, environmentally conscious wineries and growers – California's Fetzer Vineyards being perhaps the most celebrated example in

America – have in recent years shifted to sustainable or organic winegrowing. The huge Gallo enterprise is said to grow more than half of its grapes organically. A few large table grape growers in the state's Central Valley are among the group.

Although spring dampness may promote mildew even in California, fungi cannot thrive in the constant high daytime temperatures of California's summer months. The major fungus diseases are far greater threats in regions with summer rainfall and cooler temperatures. There are an estimated 6,000 grape growers in eastern America, and only three other growers to my knowledge – two in New York's Finger Lakes district and one in Virginia – are devoted to organic or sustainable methods.

At my vineyard in Scenery Hill, I did not use fungicides during the first two years. I concentrated more on improving the soil. In 1993, black rot had ruined some fruit on the few Chambourcin plants in my vineyard, but the crop was so small that the damage was not disastrous. To control the fungus, I had destroyed one by one the grapes that showed the black rot spots because the disease is spread when rain splashes fungal spores from infected berries. I was working on a small scale and have no illusion that the technique would be practical for large growers, but regardless of the vineyard, the best medicine for combatting all disease is to prevent berries, shoots, or leaves with infection spots from falling on the ground. Unless buried or otherwise disposed, the fungus will stay alive on the plant tissue and spread through the growing season, and even over the winter, to reappear the next year.

As a result of the black rot scare in 1993, I sprayed chemical fungicides twice in 1994 during May, but aimed to not spray at all after the berries were set. Infection stayed away throughout June. A little black rot showed up in mid-July – less than 5 percent of the crop was affected – but by the time the black sores had appeared on the fruit two weeks later, ripening was setting in. Most large commercial growers would not have tolerated the damage, but I was pleased enough, feeling I had struck a decent balance between chemicals and control.

I had about a ton of grapes hanging, enough for about 160 gallons of wine.

Through mid-summer, the weather was superbly warm. It was looking like a banner year for Pennsylvania Cynthiana.

AFTER MY CASUAL MENTION at Heinrich Grohe's about opening a winery, Nadine and I began talking more earnestly about the idea. She could see how devoted I was to the notion but was concerned that we didn't have the business experience to succeed. If we did it, though, she wanted to keep her job in the city, and commute.

I was less worried about not having business experience, and skeptical about finding affordable property close enough to the city that we could keep our jobs. Also, I preferred a more rural location. "I don't want to end up on the edge of the suburbs buying acreage that'll have a Wal-Mart across the road in ten years," I told Nadine. She sympathized but felt we'd have to commute for many years.

How we could ever work something out with Mrs. Weaver, to live at Scenery Hill, I just couldn't imagine. It was too far from the city, and we could not afford to buy her farm anyway, if she should ever decide to sell it. I didn't rule out Scenery Hill, but it seemed very unlikely we could ever make it work there.

In truth, Nadine was in no hurry to do anything. As 1994 wore on, though, I was. The idea had hold of me. Farming and making wine was what I wanted to do. Finding the right piece of property, I concluded, was the first step.

Spring and Summer 1994

EARLY ON IN THE 1994 GROWING SEASON, I had decided to spend much less time mowing and cutting weeds than in past years because the vines had a deep enough root system, I reasoned, to stand up to the competition for moisture and nutrients.

The best thing for the soil, I thought, was to let the grass grow. I wanted the vineyard lush and wooly, the way a "live farmer" would have it. (That's my favorite term from 1930s' novelist-turned-farmer Louis Bromfield, who used it to describe farmers who are "thinking while they're farming.") Farmers, gardeners, even urban lawn-tenders, take great pride in the way their grassy areas look, I suspect because the constant growth of weeds and grass provides an easy and obvious way to showcase personal attitudes about controlling nature. Weeds and grass grow rampantly in my vineyard. I rarely use weed-killers. The soil is spongy and crumbly, and able to sustain the plants during drought.

Because I don't use chemical insecticides, the soil is also jumping with earthworms, which have among their chores the task of bettering soil fertility. In a healthy acre, in which decomposition is always proceeding, earthworms supply many tons of their nutrient-rich manure every year.

I said earlier that green is the color of good health, but there are exceptions. A vineyard with all of its leaves green in neatly manicured vine rows with no grass around the plants, a standard image in brochures and books and film clips of many famous vineyard districts the world over, is almost always chemical-dependent; chemicals make the leaves so perfect and chemicals make the ground so bare. Australia may be the most chemically dependent winegrowing nation of all. Grapes roll to the horizon there, in 1,000-acre vineyards with nary a blade of grass in sight. As in arid districts with intensive agriculture in California, precious water cannot be wasted on grass. But it's a little bit sick that in many of those vineyards you'd be lucky to find an earthworm.

My weeds were shin-high by mid-May 1994, when I chopped them up with a rotary plow, planted a white clover cover crop, then just let whatever came up grow. The deer were in the vineyard during the first two months, nipping leaves and even the young celery-like canes here and there, but they seemed to pose no big threat. There was plenty of green growth to go around, and they rarely ate the developing grape clusters.

The transition to this hands-off approach had not come all at once. There was the Saturday in late spring 1992, right after planting, that I showed up to find many of the brand new leaves gnawed to their main veins by chomping leaf hoppers about the size of a staple. I was horrified at the damage, and immediately laid on the poison.

I hated the sweet-sour smell of the stuff as I applied it, and had a feeling it was a mistake – a vague, uncomfortable feeling is all.

I wrote a letter expressing this uncomfortable sensation to the poet/farmer/author Wendell Berry. (A woman in the English department at the University of Kentucky had said to address the letter to him in Fort Royal, Kentucky – "Don't worry, he'll get it.") A week or so later a brief hand-written note returned advising me to accept some bug and disease damage, and that after a while I would get used to accepting it, and then a little later I would probably no longer notice.

In direct contrast to the feeling I had with those chemicals was the calm of Wendell Berry.

I started by accepting the damage of little bugs, and by mid-Summer 1994 had worked my way up to mammals. I came to believe they had gotten used to me being there, and I thought we had an understanding that they could take their rightful share. I saw them watching me in the weeds and woodlots. And I certainly didn't mind the sight of the svelt doe and its fawns bounding silently down the vineyard hill into woodsy shadows when I arrived on weekend mornings.

A predilection examined earlier for scenic sunsets drew me in the evenings, too. One day in early July, when a weather front passed through in the morning and cleared the haze and hovering humidity, I drove out after work.

When I arrived at the vineyard, the sun was a roasting orange and draining away.

From my knees on the thick green mat of the vineyard, I fell back on my haunches so that the tops of the bluestem and wild timothy were at about eye level. Grasses stood tall and still and sparkly in the hayfield below the vineyard, and as I watched, more intently than ever before, I saw that every plant on the hillside – grape leaf, wildflower, weed top, mighty tree alike – was reaching, stretching upward. As far and wide as my eye could travel, plants everywhere pulled at their roots for the sky. As the sun started to slip below the horizon, leaves and wildflower petals and weed heads drooped.

There was a brief moment, right before the last sun-slice, when I scratched out a little patch of grass and leaned sideways to put my ear to the earth. There I heard. . . . What I heard was a sort of drumming. It thrilled me, welling up inside.

I stretched and rolled and rubbed. I wallowed in the soft expanse the way one may upon awakening in a luxurious bed. I lay there panting, spread-eagle, face up. When I tilted my head to the ground again, I heard the drumming . . . a sort of primal drumming. That's the only way I can describe it. It seems self-conscious only in the telling really.

Sitting up, I interpreted an immense orchestration, and though the day was done, not an ending. And though something personal was promised, it was not for me alone.

A wisp of wind from somewhere stirred, from nowhere I could see. I waited and watched the sun colors pass. Moments, seconds, minutes later, the cool of white – an iridescent white – was upon the land.

AN INTEREST in the more complicated workings of the natural world, and my place in it began in farming in 1992 but had not enveloped me, I can say now, until the spring of 1994.

Driving across Ten Mile Creek in southeastern Washington County that May, I noted that Ten Mile looked like a promising spot for bluegill, the perch-type fish I'd loved to catch as a kid in Missouri. A tree had fallen across part of the stream, obstructing the main current and creating backwater areas that fish love. I had not been fishing in twenty years, but the next time I went to the vineyard, a license, pole, reel and worms were with me. I planned the day to include a couple of hours before dark for fishing.

On the way to the creek, I stopped off at a spring down the road 3 miles from the grapes. It's the opposite direction from home for me, but I had begun to take the ten-minute detour anyway, to relax and fill a few jugs. (You cannot believe the homemade beer from this water!)

The spring gushes out between a honey locust and two walnut trees, just off the road; cars pull up right beside.

Across the blacktop, a farmer lets cows roam his steep ground, and as with so many of America's rural hillsides, beef cattle are this land's ruination. It is the farmer's fault, not the cows': cattle eat the grass, and expose the steep barren ground to their heavy hooves. Then comes the rain and wind to loosen and carry soil downhill. What started as a muddy trickle at the bottom of the hill grows into a stream that rages during thunderstorms and eats away further at the hill. Eventually gullies form, and still the farmer lets the cows roam. Then the next rain comes, and look! – there goes our topsoil to the Gulf of Mexico.

It is said that more than half of America's original topsoil has been squandered through bad farming practices in only about a century and a half of intensive white man farming.

In this Washington County valley, the spring side of the hill strikes a dramatic contrast to the cattle side. A gradual slope of hayfield rises above the spring, and the man who owns the land has allowed a little shaded "facility" to be created. At the spring, there are pipes, thigh-high off the ground, jutting from the hillside cranny, and a rock-lined basin under the pipes.

In spring, the frigid water gushes out to fill a gallon jug in under ten seconds. Even at the spring's lowest ebb in the driest summer, a gallon never takes more than a minute.

People come from all around to get their drinking water, and have for a long time (the byway being named "Spring Valley Road"). One man there the day I went fishing said he'd raised four children on the water. With each of the fifteen or twenty jugs that he filled, he became more elated in talking about the water's goodness. Twenty-eight years he'd been coming, he said. "We use it for everything, coffee and all. This's the sweetest."

He ran his hand through the clear jet, feeling the water, letting it caress him.

It was an unusually warm May Saturday, and wrinkles on my face were lined with salt and soil crust. After he left and I made sure no one was coming up the road, I stripped and slithered around on the wet rocks under the torrent for maybe a minute, yelping at the iciness on my hot skin. I lathered quickly with the soap I'd brought and rinsed, yelping less and less as my skin adjusted to the artesian cold.

In fresh clothes, I lolled around in the shade, air-drying. Waves of heat wafted from my head.

I batted my eyes in the faint breeze as my tuxedo cat Ed does in a window breeze, and rolled onto my back. Then I was aware of my own small smile, felt it with my fingertips.

This was when I began to seriously consider living in the country.

Always before, I had just figured I would grow grapes and put up a winery somewhere in the area, but that we would continue living in the city. What followed that May evening – going fishing right after being flash-cooled and rejuvenated – I often long for in the middle of summer work weeks. Now I go fishing as often as I can. And I bathe in that spring almost every time I work at the vineyard. And I'm much closer than ever to a life in the country.

One outdoor activity like fishing quickly led to others that added a new dimension to being "outside." A friend who lived a half-hour from the vineyard wanted to do a little fishing, too, so he and I would hook up on evenings after work, or on my rare weekends that didn't include vineyard work. To involve Nadine, not much into fishing, I suggested a hike before or after the fishing part. Before long, we were going on weekend hikes with no fishing. In June, we went camping one Saturday in a wilderness area up in the Laurel Mountains 70 miles east of Pittsburgh. I loved it up there in the mountains. Nadine loved it. We went again.

I began to read Thoreau and John Muir and John Burroughs and then Aldo Leopold's *A Sand County Almanac*, and many other things.

Pretty soon, we were camping the year-round. We hiked into state forest wilderness in Fayette County with friends and built a sweat lodge of saplings draped with blankets. Two among us with engineering bents dammed the mountain stream rushing past the campsite, creating a pool about 5 feet deep and 20 feet across. On one glorious late summer Saturday, cooler than usual, there was a full moon. We did our sweating – rocks heated by fire and placed in a pit, us surrounding it in the center of the "lodge" – and then we tumbled out, time after time, four hours' worth, to run down to the stream, where we'd jump in and sling wet hair in the moonlight and howl like coyotes from the water-shock. The moonglow that lit our way from lodge to stream shimmered smack in the middle of the rushing current.

The next morning, we swam more and then put all the rocks back, restoring the run's original course.

I collected several stones of limestone and sandstone with stripes of other rock types and, back home, laid them on magazines on our dining room table. I enjoyed looking at each of them all week long.

We have gone there dozens of times now. Summer full moons are particularly wonderful. The centered moon creates an oddly formal setting on the big rock as we sit in the stream middle where the whitecaps glisten. Once, as clouds came and went across October's full moon, a friend sighted Saturn with the small telescope, big as a bazooka, which he had packed in. In chiffon-colored moonlight, high in the mountains, we watched Saturn's rings in the quick cloud-breaks.

Since returning to some association with the rural hills and deep forests, I have been growled away from stream crossings at midnight by red, hopping bear eyes. I know the primal shriek of the red-tail hawk and the screech owl's keening. I have found turkey vulture chicks in their nest while a nervous mother the size of a 767 circled and swooped overhead. Where before I heard only the blaring city, I now sit beside tumbling waters in the West Virginia mountains for hours, listening and watching.

I have become a passably good trout fisherman with cheapo spinning tackle and worms. I spend nearly every peak weekend in the spring and fall, weather permitting, in the country and the woods. Nadine and I usually camp a couple of times on clear winter weekends, and three or four times in April and May. Our absolute favorite outdoor activity is cross-country skiing.

When we go on vacations, we search out stands of virgin forest, wilderness tracts, native prairie areas, or seaside salt marshes near our destinations. It is fair to say that our lives, to some degree, revolve around the natural world and our desire to understand its influence on human beings better. Often, natural features determine our destinations. We hike most weekends during warm weather; the summertime Saturday or Sunday afternoon not spent in the wilds, one way or another, is rare. We try to cook a meal outdoors whenever we can: sometimes on Friday after work, we gather up simple foods and a little wine, drive seventy-five minutes to the Allegheny Mountains, and hike into the woods a few hundred yards to cook a dinner under the stars on a Mexican blanket.

And just what else was learned? From vineyard work and outdoor hours, I know the schedules of flowering for the most common weeds, the breeding cycle and nesting habits of the redwinged blackbirds which keep my company in the fields ringing the vineyard. I watch them dive into the alfalfa and I occasionally break from the work to wade into the grass to see their brown-speckled eggs in cleverly hidden nests. The birds call wildly and fly to another

The author in Jacks Fork River, Ozark Mountains, 1997.

area, trying to decoy me.

I have down the times of emergence and basic behavior of numerous insects. I can tell a berry moth's puncture wound on my grapes from a stinkbug's.

Why do sycamore trees – I've seen them growing exactly the same on my street in Pittsburgh as in the woodlot below my vines, or on Monterey Peninsula a football field away from the ocean, or lining the lane of wine chateaux in France – drop one-fifth of their leaves in mid-summer?

I went to the library to learn that if a single goose flies within twenty yards of the human ear on a still spring evening, chances are high that it lost its lifelong mate to a hunter the fall before.

THE MORE I PICKED UP "in the field," the more I wanted to read. I found that the benefits and enjoyment of practical experience were heightened a lot by reading.

In a parallel universe to the Harvard University scientist E.O. Wilson's "biophilia," which he describes as the human tendency "to focus on life and life-like processes" when an interest in biodiversity is somehow sparked, I uncovered truths from Aldo Leopold, another man with a scientific bent who is also America's most revered twentieth century environmental writer. In an obscure 1923 essay, "Some Fundamentals of Conservation in the Southwest," Leopold wrote: "Possibly in our intuitive perceptions, which may be truer than our science and less impeded by words than our philosophies, we realize the indivisibility of the earth – its soil, mountains, rivers, forest, climate, plants, and animals – and respect it collectively not only as a useful servant but as a living being, vastly less alive than ourselves, but vastly greater than ourselves in time and space."

Time and space are not clever aphorisms. I believe Leopold, as many others before him and since, used those words because they have great significance in non-Christian mysticism. For many aboriginal people in many different parts of the world, nature worship alters perceptions of time and space, and is a central pillar in their spiritual belief system.

Once I started to make such connections, I also found it nearly impossible to locate an interested ear. I started to express my ideas only in letters to my mother. In many ways, I told her, it seemed as if my "conversion" was following some pattern that I would only later come to perceive. Comprehension often lags, I've noticed. She had lost most of her eyesight to diabetes, but a half-continent away she still managed to scribble back words of encouragement or questions that spurred me on.

A few weeks before she died in December 1993, she called and asked that I tell her the story again about the life of the vine – "the one you sent in your letter," she said, "with the birds and the blackening rot."

I keep copies of correspondence, and was able to dig it out as we chatted.

"I have it now, Mom. Here goes: 'So, if it survives a torrid, wind-blasted winter, then makes it through April and early May without frost killing everything to the ground, then survives black rot in May and June, then isn't hit by high winds, driving rain, or hail during the period that it is flowering and setting berries (which happens to be the same time that such storms are most common), then is spared the insect disasters of July and August, it can look forward to battling the birds for every last fruit of its production in September and October.'"

"That story," she said, "makes me see how the odds are stacked against a plant. And against you, too."

Birds were the least of my harvest problems in 1994.

I could have used my mother's comfort.

"Harvest" 1994

TURNING BLUE IN AUGUST, the grapes catch the attention of animals which start to monitor the ripening nuggets. Besides birds, there are deer, raccoons, opossums, and foxes to eat the grapes. Nylon mesh netting offers some protection, but it's expensive and aggravating to get in place. I netted half of my rows during the first week of September, with harvest less than two weeks away. Grass and weeds in the aisles were waist-deep, and it is was so enchanting to wade through this lush green wave, stop occasionally, and fondle hand-sized bunches of bulging berries.

While putting on the netting, I had noticed clusters with big bites out of them, and had blamed deer. I never saw a raccoon, fox or opossum in the vineyard, and with the vegetation so tall, neither could the horned owl or the hawk, their major predators.

But the damage was tolerable. Let them eat a few grapes, I said to myself, for I have a ton of them. Let them all eat a few of the grapes that I have worked since last winter to raise. I was so thrilled with my accomplishments.

That was on a Thursday evening. Not the Saturday two days later, but the following Saturday, in the late afternoon, Nadine came along with me. It had been an unseasonably warm week, so we took clippers, just in case the very ripest bunches needed to be picked, but mainly I went to check in and to do a rough measure of their sugar content. I was figuring that harvest was still at least a week away.

We walked into the vineyard and immediately noticed that vines on the outside edges had no grapes dangling. Going deeper into the vineyard revealed the same. From the center of row 3, in the middle of the hill, we looked in all directions for a grape.

The urge to run wildly from one corner of the vineyard to the other struck me to the core, but faltering after a few confused steps, there was no reason: we could see all there was: every single grape was gone. The bunches were picked clean and clinging by their stems like skeletons to the vines, by the hundreds. Even inside the netting, the bunches were skeletons, the berries methodically pulled from their stems and eaten grape after grape after grape after grape.

Beside Nadine, I turned woozy. My legs gave out, I sank to my knees in the tall grass. All across the hill, the skeletons hung from the vines.

I looked at her eyes roaming, straining to see this . . . this absence. I could look only at her then, so that I saw every movement of her neck muscles and shoulder and her forearm and hand – how, without turning and while murmuring, "Oh, Paul," it came to my shoulder. I watched her hand there for the longest time.

~seven~

THANKSGIVING TIME is when Nadine and I make our annual trip to Missouri to see my family. It's always a fun week of road travel and relaxation, but in 1994, by the time we reached the interminable flatness of Interstate 70 that begins in western Ohio, I was ready to turn tail for home. Preoccupied then – it may sound melodramatic now – I felt severe conflict about whether I was competent to make a living away from the city. And four states and fourteen hours behind the wheel seemed like more time than I needed to replay fall's events.

Autumn is my favorite season, and we make it a time of revelry and plenty. We throw parties, press wine with friends in the backyard, hike and camp and take advantage of the remaining warmth outdoors. The most memorable emotion in '94, however, was embarrassment from having to explain to everyone who knew about my vineyard venture what had happened.

Each personal contact seemed to re-bruise my battered attitude. Tense and discouraged, I mainly didn't speak unless spoken to.

To make matters worse, I am not someone who automatically responds, "Oh, everything's fine," when people ask, "How's it going?"

I watched their eyes widen at my pathetic vintage report, and I saw their eyes harden when I came to my excuses for failing. "Right," I imagined them saying as they walked away, "animals ate everything."

This year, I didn't find the interstate billboard near Columbus promoting "America's Largest Community of Homes" and the pre-fab houses stretching to the horizon very amusing; no, the seven-story office building in the actual shape of a picnic basket near Newark, Ohio, didn't affect me in 1994.

And I knew that once we got to Missouri, there would be a new round of describing how I had worked for three years at growing grapes and had nothing to show for it.

I've always been known as a "serious kind of guy," but one reason I took this matter so seriously was that I was, after all, looking for land on which to build a winery. I planned to make a living as a winegrower. In all stages of learning to grow grapes, I calculated whether what I was doing in miniature was practical on a commercial scale.

I discarded many ideas proven too labor-intensive or otherwise ineffective. I once tried to keep deer out of the vineyard by laying several hundred feet of scavenged chain link fence on the ground, thinking it might serve as a sort of "deer grate," like a cattle grate made of metal, which keeps the animals from crossing.

Animals don't like walking on steel, and a deer would also be afraid of catching its hoofed feet, I reasoned. Dumb idea, dumb for several reasons. It worked fairly well keeping deer out, but when the grass grew up through the fence, I had no good way to maintain it: can't run a lawnmower across chain link fence; hard to weedwhack it very short; obstructed passage of equipment on all sides, for fear of catching the edge of the fence on a tiller tine or mower blade. Just a mess of an idea.

The point had been to find a fairly inexpensive, low-tech fix. After that, I went straight for the electric fence with a battery charger, 3 wires, compound-like – not real pretty but I had to keep the deer out. Little was often not practical.

I thought longterm a lot – you can't think about the future too much, right? – and the loss I felt at Thanksgiving in 1994, I thought, would hound me forever.

The people of Scenery Hill figured in, as well. Having spent a few dozen days a year, most weekends three years in a row at the Weaver farm, had brought me into contact with a lot of people in the area. I stopped at the farm supply, quickstops, bars, and hardware stores around the vineyard in Washington County. My friends worked at a commercial pottery in Scenery Hill. I got to know a few of the local celebrities, and most people were curious about what I was doing. Word spread surprisingly fast by mouth alone.

"Oh, you're the grape man," they'd say. "How's it going out there?"

Due to the '94 harvest debacle, that became a sickening question to hear. All I could think about was living in the country surrounded by these country people, and feeling my own family frying beneath pryin' eyes.

I thought also how obviously three seasons of winegrowing had revealed, above all, that I was a novice; an enthusiastic novice. I had a few months' apprenticeship in wine, and I'd attended a couple of seminars. Then I'd started a little vineyard, with the aim of making it much bigger.

Now it turned out I didn't know what I was doing, which, in reality, could well have been true all along. That's it. That was the situation.

"So long, loser, maybe we'll see you next year," I envisioned everyone saying behind my back.

Imagine, I kept thinking, if I had a winery and did this for a living. Such a failure with a commercial-sized vineyard and a winery might crush my family.

Thankfully, concentrated grief has a way of playing itself out, and along about central Illinois, cruising mind-numbing Interstate 70 across a bleak early winter prairie, the meaning of the harvest failure to which I had been privileged started to sink in.

I did, after all, still have a job. The serious threat was to the future – not now. One can think too much about the future, I realized, for amidst great bitterness it also seemed abundantly clear that between Spring 1992 and Fall 1994 experience in farming had privileged me to peculiar insights. In tragedy, it is said, there is also opportunity. As for viniculture in western Pennsylvania, in the late twentieth century with not a lot of money to spend, I had learned that a particular sort of wisdom may be gained only in the doing.

From I-70, we struck diagonally south and still west on Interstate 57, through the oil and gas fields of southern Illinois, vent fires flaming like Saudi Arabia.

At the junction of the Ohio and Mississippi rivers, where three states come together around Cairo, Illinois, we lumbered up on to U.S. 62's old two-lane bridge. It must be two miles long, crossing part of a fertile river delta that rivals the Nile's at Alexandria. The soil is a yard deep and the color of coal, for corn and soybeans and, used to be, some cotton. A person grows garden cauliflower there the size of basketballs, prize tomatoes, calf-sized watermelons.

Looking down to the right on the Kentucky side, looking way down – a virtual diorama it was, so high above the sprawling flood plain – a farm machine inched across a field of corn stubble, and black soil flowed behind, burying the frail browns of a finished season. A light speck rode the tiny tractor.

Nadine caught my eye going back and forth from bridge lane to blackening field, and said, "What are you looking at so hard?"

I said something to the effect that it was really some sight to see. I said nothing really. I'd seen farmers working those fields eighty miles from my hometownof Poplar Bluff a dozen times over the years; that's mostly, though not all, what I was pondering.

In fact, it was very plain – too plain to waste words on. After a moment, I glanced at her and, feeling invigoration in my chest and trying to convey to her the weight which was lifting, I said: "I've just never seen it at Thanksgiving time, Beautiful."

Early Winter 1995

LATE JANUARY, during the first warmup of the winter, four months after the apocalypse, was when I returned to my Scenery Hill vineyard.

Earlier in the month, I had researched raccoons and deer at the library, and talked to a few Washington County hunters and other wildlife authorities on the phone.

Once the 1995 growing season began, I decided, I would try to keep the deer out with chainlink fencing laid on the ground along the perimeter of the vineyard. Such a fear fools cattle at a fence gate, so maybe, I reckoned, it would work for deer. Slave to the picturesque, I did not want to give my beloved hillside a penitentiary look with vertical fencing.

The growing season came, and the fence in the grass kept the deer out at first. But by mid-May, they had it figured and were eating a lot of leaves and developing clusters – serious damage. In early June, I put up the lightweight, 3-wire, electrified vertical fence about 5 feet high, on flexible fiberglass poles. Powered by a 12-volt marine battery, it can't harm a deer, but it was supposed to scare them when they touched it.

Coming out of the vineyard one afternoon, I met Mrs. Weaver hanging wash. "Ain't seen a man come from the mines looking dirtier'n you," she said as I approached. Sweat had turned the dust to mud smears on my T-shirt. I was proud when she asked, "How's it going, farmer?"

As we chatted, I could tell that Mrs. Weaver was going to share with me some insider information. She had a crafty manner of leading up to the real question with polite queries about the mundane. She and her son Lou had been talking again, I could tell.

"Heard you wired yourself up a little short fence," she finally said, squinting into the hot mid-day sun and holding back a laugh. "Why, they'll jump right over that. Deer can jump in the air, you know."

My face flushed. "The guy down at Buckeye Feed said cattle ranchers use it," I stammered, "and he'd heard it works on deer."

He instructed me to lure the deer to the fence with a spot of peanut butter. "Once they get a mouthful of that," I advised Mrs. Weaver, "why, they learn their lesson. Oh, they won't come back then. They'll be too afraid to get near it, to jump over."

She squinted at me again. "Why, they'll jump right over that," she repeated.

But the fence worked, and within a few weeks, word had gotten around. "And how many wire is it?" the owner of Scenery Hill Hardware had inquired. "And they don't jump over?" A little clot of men at the register leaned an ear in as I explained.

Raccoons proved to be far more intractable. I never did see a raccoon in the vines, but only they could have pried open the netting. The wildlife authorities had said that constant trapping and an electric fence at 6 inches off the ground were the only sure-fire methods for detouring raccoons from ripe fruit.

My brother had said killing them was the only hope. "You'll never keep them out," he warned. "You can't beat a raccoon, you can only kill him."

"What about," I asked everyone so urgent to share their best advice, "keeping the grass cut so that the hawks and owls have a good shot at them?" Experts from the hunters' lobby laughed at the notion. But a specialist at a federal Agriculture Department office in Harrisburg, Pennsylvania, said there was a good chance that good "vineyard hygiene" would help. "Unless the population is just out of control, creating conditions suitable for predation might be sufficient to control raccoons. But you probably should be prepared to accept some loss of crop every year."

Like all predators, birds of prey concentrate on the young, old and feeble for their kills, and the birds can take enough young raccoons especially to suppress the adult population. The fear of predation is often enough to detour small animals from open areas.

In addition, I learned, not all raccoons overdue the fruit course.

"That was probably the work of a few greedy individuals," said one authority at Pennsylvania's Department of Environmental Resources. "Really, most raccoons wouldn't gorge themselves like that, night after night. You had the bad luck to run up against some irresponsible ones."

Still another thing I learned about farming in 1995 was how to raise Cynthiana vines from cuttings with a high rate of success. First, I selected cuttings from my fall prunings in which there were junctions of 2-year-old and 1-year-old wood. Cynthiana had a peculiar tendency, I had noticed over the years, to form numerous small buds around such junctions. Above ground, these buds make superfluous leafy growth; underground, I thought, this superfluous growth would multiply by many times the possibility of roots forming on a buried shoot. It is the same idea as rooting plants through layering, discussed in chapter 2, but much easier to carry out in the field.

I also had read about the trick in a Civil War-era horticulture manual. I didn't know anyone doing it nowadays, but maybe the technique was well-known in the 1860s. Maybe it was common forty years before that. Perhaps Dr. D.N. Norton of Richmond, Virginia, did it.

So, in April of 1995, I buried about 175 such cuttings. More than 80 percent "took." I could use them and others made in the same fashion when I planted a new vineyard in years ahead, thus saving the cost of buying rooted cuttings from a nursery. I was proud.

Vintage time came in '95, and the fence worked against the deer and to a lesser extent against the raccoons. It was a cool, rainy year, and I harvested about 1,500 pounds of somewhat underripe Cynthiana grapes. I was getting into the swing of things.

AS LATE AS 1930, in the vast part of the continent between the Rocky Mountains and the industrial East, a reigning majority of people lived on farms. My parents were the first generation of kids to grow up entirely in a town. But their parents, just one generation back, were reared in the country: sons and daughters of subsistence farmers, my peoples' ancestors came to the region one or two generations earlier, locked hold of a piece of land, and hung on. Countless others – the majority, in fact – never owned rural property; they worked for those who did, and rented.

They hunted wild game, tended a garden and maybe a few fruit trees, raised some livestock, and grew a little corn to fatten hogs and for distilling into whiskey, which provided "their brief periods of entertainment," as one modern account puts it. My people doubtlessly led an often desperate existence not unlike what Americans hear today of rural Africa or South America.

Most of these pioneers' offspring originated in Scotland or Germany, and, upon hitting America's shores, first lived in Pennsylvania, Maryland, and Virginia, before moving further west. In my family's case (on one side, anyway), the next stop was southern Illinois. Typically, it had taken these German and Celtic immigrants a generation or so in the East to hear of cheap land and a social structure still coalescing in the continent's midsection that might provide an opening for them.

Migrants to the farmlands of the Midwest usually had no serious interest in farming, much less know-how. By the time their children, or children of their children, were coming of age in the early twentieth century, the exodus to the city from America's farms and smallest farm villages was in full swing.

Jobs for cash in factory towns and railroad hubs and in the big cities churning out the early products of a consumer society lured my grandparents and their generation away. Most likely preferred a bare-bulb room in the city to the tortures of life on a farm, where the yeoman tradition I am so fond of glamorizing, in central Missouri, for instance, was actually scarce. Most farmers were not yeomen. John Graves, writing in the early 1970s about the "hard scrabble" life in West Texas scrub country that he chose, traces "a great deal of articulate revulsion against rural things and ways" to this peculiar past. "Not many years ago, nearly all American towns and cities teemed with people whose general optimism and drive were fueled by vast joy at having escaped 'the farm.'"

My mother's mother, for instance, moved from the farm to work at a box factory all her life in Poplar Bluff. The only raise she ever received was when the minimum wage went up, and she was *in the union.*

My maternal grandfather was reared by poor parents on an Illinois farm. Then there was my dad's dad, Carl Roberts, who died in 1995. As a teen, he "followed the wheat harvest," he was fond of telling me. "We started in Texas in a hundred degrees and ended in Nebraska in snow up to your belt buckle." He lived as a vagabond, eating whatever his crew of young men and younger women, brothers and sisters and acquaintances, could scrape together on a few cents a day. They'd sleep in haystacks through harvest, or until they could go no deeper into winter with their light coats. I don't know what he did immediately after that, but he said he saved his first nickel working in the auto industry and living in a Detroit boarding house. By the late 1920s, he was back in Poplar Bluff, looking for work.

By the early '30s, he was married to a local girl and was a gas man, walking town reading meters. During the Depression, gas company executives cut everybody's salary by 50 percent – everybody's, as Carl Roberts tells it, but his. "Most of those men couldn't do anything," Granddad said, "being straight off the farm with no education, no skills."

When Carl objected during the announcement of the pay cut that "gas was a new business" and that times had never been better in the industry, the suits ordered the pay cuts effective immediately, told him they'd see him in the back room, and hastily closed the meeting. In the back room, they threatened to fire him, but he said he pointed out there wasn't a man on the force who did his job as quickly, and that if they wanted him to stay on they'd give him a dime an hour raise.

Within three years, in the belly of the Depression, he had saved enough money to buy a plumbing and heating business, still owned today by my family. My father and his mother and brother grew up in the post-war boom years. My grandfather made quite a bit of money, was a local politician of some renown, and was flying a private plane by 1953. "Soloed before my wife ever knew I was taking lessons," he used to crow.

Born on a small farm plot outside of town, in an area where men with no farming sense had let their livestock roam and defoliate the hillsides so much that a lot of the Ozarks' topsoil had washed away to underlying rock, in a few years choking nearly every bend in once beautiful swift rivers with gravel, Granddad had ended up with piped gas in a modest home on North 12th Street. His beautiful wife, Edith (beautiful to this day at over 85), from a similar background – lightning killed a relative of hers as he chopped wood on the home place in the hills north of Poplar Bluff – was plenty pleased to trade country air for a gas range and a Fridgidaire. I've seen the pictures.

In a span of roughly forty years, one generation, America went from predominantly farmers and farmtown folk to a nation of city-living factory workers. From a vantage point still in our own century, and considering the immensity of the revolution, there seems to be little mass regret. In many countries, distrust between country and city people figures mightily in class tensions and cultural discourse, but not so in America. I think of French and Italian neo-realist films – the longing for pre-war rural simplicity in Federico Fellini's "La Dolce Vita" – or the literary career of Englishman John Berger, who for the last two decades has probably written more – fiction and non-fiction, academic and popular – than anyone about the rural peasantry of western Europe and how rural folkways and traditions still influence European life.

But, just barely beyond the consciousness of my generation, my grandparents and those of nearly everyone with whom I grew up were farmers, yet I cannot lead anyone to the land outside town where my grandparents lived.

ONE COLD JANUARY SATURDAY in Pennsylvania, I squealed to a stop in front of a vacant eighteenth-century stone house with a gnarly catalpa tree and a realtor's sign in the front yard. A call to the Uniontown realtor revealed the property also included the steep, 6-acre wooded hillside rising directly behind the home. Its location in Fayette County only 3 miles from heavily traveled U.S. 40 – the National Road, the country's first publicly financed highway west from the Eastern Seaboard, laid in the early 1800s and now a major tourism route – was just about ideal as a winery spot. The hill would have to be cleared for the vineyard, but the site was pretty good:

south-facing, thin limestone-laced soil, about 900 feet above sea level.

"How long did it take you to get back?" was Nadine's first question when I burst into the house with the news.

"Rats," I said. I had been so excited, calculating vine rows and the sun's angle on them that I hadn't even kept track of the time while driving. "I knew there was something. . . ."

Our trip to meet the realtor the next afternoon took 70 minutes – a tolerable commute, we figured, for a few years anyway. The old home needed loads of work, including new roof trusses and a roof, and we'd have to construct a separate winery building, but at the price we offered, we could pull it off. When the out-of-town owners accepted four days later, we felt sure that a vineyard chiseled out of a hill above a stately stone house-winery would be a memorable stop for travelers on the National Road.

Negotiations to the close the transaction dragged on for several weeks. Acquiring the property was in jeopardy. The house was central to a bitter divorce settlement, and each partner claimed ownership. Liens and lawyers had to be satisfied, and no one on their side was in any hurry.

We, on the other hand, were. Since our purchase offer had been accepted, the owners in the end would be obligated to sell, so I wrangled an agreement to begin cutting trees on the hillside while the legal wrinkles were ironed out. A friend who owned a similar rural rock house 5 miles away was pleased to imagine us living nearby, and graciously helped me on three straight weekends. Chainsaws roared. I ordered vines to plant. I found a contractor willing to stand by ready to rebuild the roof, our downpayment given with the contingency it would be returned if the deal dissolved. I ordered new windows and doors, and arranged for delivery of a tile roof. Everything was ready to go for a mid-April closing.

The phone rang about 7:15 a.m. on a Sunday morning in mid-March. "Mr. Roberts," said Morton Rosenstein, the realtor, "the stone house burned down overnight."

All that remained of the home Jonathan Miller built in 1783 beside Redstone Creek were its four walls of rock quarried one ridge over. Police and fire investigators at first wondered if lightning during a thunderstorm sparked the fire, but a few days later, crime lab technicians ended the speculation. An accelerant had started the fire.

Arson.

Over a two-year period, more than 25 families in Fayette County had lost homes to arsonists whom police believed operated as a ring. A motive was not apparent. "We know who set your fire," an investigator told me the day lab reports came in, "but just like all the others, there's no good reason for it." He said those responsible were just "fire freaks."

"We just can't get any evidence to arrest. They're sticking together. We have an informant who says they're mainly teenagers, led by one older boy, and that they're devil-worshippers, or some such thing. We're waiting for one of them to break off and talk on the others, but so far. . . ."

In fact, the suspects in the fires, all in rural areas of the county, lived less than 1 mile away from the stone house.

With the best feature of the property gone, and ownership still in dispute, the purchase could not be consummated.

To this day, the smoke-stained walls of the historic home still stand beside the catalpa tree. The whole valley seems still to mourn, for structures so lived-in possess spirits. To this day, the unscrupulous contractor still has our downpayment. To this day, Nadine and I cannot talk about the episode without faltering.

The days and weeks that followed passed as a sickening blur. Bud-break came and went in the vineyard. Doubts about a future as a winegrower haunted me. It was two months before I could muster the mind-set to plod out to the vineyard and farm again.

We had visited dozens of farms and "farmettes," in practically every county ringing Pittsburgh. One winter, we spent practically every spare minute traveling snow-slickened backroads, talking to landowners, and searching for realty signs. Now it was Summer 1996, and it seemed I was starting all over again in the search for a place in the country to have a winery.

GOOD SCHOLARLY treatments abound for anyone interested in the nation's transformation from rural to urban. But an aspect seldom addressed is the strong link between the country's agricultural heritage and the present-day renewal of interest in the natural environment.

Surely, in addressing this controversial subject, it can be agreed that the "green revival" is real.

A synthesis of the literature on farming and the literature on ecological thought (popularly called "nature writing") – the two broad subjects that I spent a few hundred hours reading about in the mid-1990s and learning about in the far larger world beyond books – exposes many overlapping themes. And it is among these themes that I will finish my intellectual peregrinations.

Michael Bunce, in a 1995 book which I rely on for parts of the skeleton of this discussion, proposes that "nature, or more accurately, the objects of nature which make up a pleasing natural scene, has long been the counterpoint of reaction against the city . . . the dichotomy between the natural and the artificial, between the works of God and those of man":

> In ancient Greek and Roman culture, and of course in the creationist foundations of the Judeo-Christian tradition, this was largely expressed in metaphorical terms. Yet classical pastoralism . . . was also influenced by the actual experience of the sights and sounds of nature. From this imaginary and experiential mix, nature emerged as the defining focus of the theme of retreat from the civilized world. This reappears in the rise of post-Medieval urban society; in the revival of literary pastoralism and in a growing attraction to nature as a source of pleasure. For the most part, however, it was the objects of nature – birds, trees, flowers, streams – which were the main source of attraction. The anthropocentric Renaissance mind, however, had a hierarchical view of the world which placed nature in an inferior position to that of human civilization. There was little interest in nature for its own sake; wild nature, in particular, evinced fear and loathing. As a source of pleasure, therefore, nature was placed in the detached and selective setting of the garden and the farm.

The Enlightenment was an age of innovation in both technology and philosophy. Many modern scholars are indebted to Clarence Glacken, who in his 1960s study notes that "in no other preceding age had thinkers discussed questions of nature and environment with such thoroughness and penetration." Yet, at the very moment that literate white Europeans in North America were hearing new metaphysical proposals about human relationships, mainly from works published on the European continent, the marginalizing of indigenous peoples in the Americas was in full swing.

What's odd is that many of the land's earlier inhabitants had lived for eons using an extension of the concepts just taking shape in the minds of the Enlightenment's intellectual "pioneers." Almost all histories by white authors of the ideas and systems later termed "ecology" and, still later, "environmentalism," avoid this irony. Yet, the Americas' native people, taken as a whole, though persecuted as backward primitives and spiritual heretics, purposefully infected with disease, starved, herded, impounded and slaughtered, were more advanced in their desire for humans to tread lightly in their environment than our civilization may ever reasonably imagine becoming. Certainly some Sioux hunters were known to slaughter and waste buffalo with a fervor attributed more commonly to white hunters, and most indigenous populations did not achieve environmental stasis. Certainly most did not, or could not, handle over-population of their lands any better than European civilizations. But all in all, it's small wonder that in the 1990s Bill Yellowtail of the Crow tribe could write: "Ecosystem protection. Sustainability. Environmental democracy. Right. Finally you're getting it."

The Eurocentric slant of the "great breakthroughs" in western thought about what may loosely be called environmental philosophy should be kept in mind when the written record is considered. The Swedish botanist Carolus Linnaeus, in his seventeenth century efforts to identify and name species, took pains to note that nature includes humans. But it fell to eighteenth century thinkers to attack an idea furthered even by Linnaeus that God's grand design was for humans to dominate all other life. Ever since, principal theorizing about the natural world has proceeded roughly along either a "mechanistic" path or one that sees nature as more like a functioning organism.

One clear consequence of the Enlightenment/Christian/anti-pagan model was the formulation of methods and classifications in the life sciences. And a consequence of these developments was that natural history became both a popular hobby and a professional field. Gilbert White's

Natural History of Selbourne, said by some to be the first great piece of nature writing, is also perhaps the best example of natural history's allure during the period.

Further refinements in western notions of "nature" are attributed to men such as David Hume, Immanuel Kant, and Jean-Jacques Rousseau (though there are philosophers who would say that implications for ecology in any of these men's work were largely accidental, and that none wrote directly about environmental philosophy). As Bunce points out, Hume commented on the internal efficiencies of the ecosystem, while Kant took up Linnaeus' point to firmly seat humans within nature, as opposed to the post-Enlightenment notion of separating humans and organisms "in the wild" into distinct spheres with infrequent contact. Rousseau, a political philosopher, branched out to argue that human fulfillment was dependent on living harmoniously with other organisms. What some westerners grasped, though hardly revolutionary by aboriginal standards, was the interdependency of actors in the natural order.

By the middle and late nineteenth century, Charles Darwin's propositions about a self-regulating natural organism had started to provoke concern about the limits implied for an industrial civilization intent on ultimate progress through science and technology. In Darwin's works, the philosophies of ecology and of the current environmental movement may be glimpsed: profound adjustments were prescribed to protect us from our industrialized selves.

There was also a growing appreciation of the significance of wilderness in the human experience (Indians excepted). Popular preferences for nature had gravitated as early as the late eighteenth century toward seeking delight and awe. As industrialization proceeded, fascination with nature's sublime powers began to infuse high art pursuits such as poetry, literature, and painting, first in England and later in North America.

"What all this led to was a wilderness cult," Michael Bunce explains, which is best exemplified by the work of English romantic poets such as William Blake and above all, Wordsworth. Nature was for humans to "experience" – a lofty and mysterious state, with a return afterward to a workaday world of order and logic. Often organized as travel excursions by boat and coach, such brief escapes from the problems of industrialism to the Scottish

Lake District or the Alps also offered a growing middle class in Europe the chance for a new cultural experience.

"Nature" was a place by now in which humans by their own decision only visited; they hardly figured within it.

In North America, alongside a desire to tame and exploit natural resources, a growing reverence for wilderness drew on English Romanticism. Trend-setters William Cullen Bryant, James Fenimore Cooper, Ralph Waldo Emerson, Henry Thoreau, and the landscape painter Thomas Cole were all heavy readers of the English "Lake poets." Most of all, Emerson and Thoreau combined elements of Plato's idealism and eastern mysticism in a search for inner peace with Wordsworth's faith in the spirituality of consorting with non-humans and natural forces.

Emerson is said to have first broached the topic at lectures in Boston in the 1830s. For three decades, he was the titular head of transcendentalism, and its prime intellectual force. Many of Emerson's ideas about humans and their only planet are remarkably similar to some attributed to Native American society leaders trying to resist the savaging of their cultures. Many of these leaders followed a nature-based spiritual code. Discussions of transcendentalism mostly omit links to the spiritual tenets of contemporary Native cultures. But certainly by the 1850s, speeches by important Native American leaders, especially during government land negotiations with various Plains Indian representatives in Washington, D.C., received extensive coverage in eastern newspapers.

Seattle, a chief and intellectual leader for several Puget Sound societies, delivered dozens of addresses to explorers, trappers, and politicians during these years. His comment to one such gathering that "even the rocks that seem to lie dumb . . . thrill with memories of past events connected with the fate of my people" is fairly representative of the argument that Native Americans made to U.S. authorities who were deciding the fate of cherished homelands. Aboriginal people tended to talk about rocks and trees symbolically, as being part of an immense spirit garden, while an interest "in the objects of nature – birds, trees, flowers, streams," as Bunce puts it, is what whites meant when they professed interest in wild things.

Thoreau, deeply worried by the mounting materialism of industrial society, picked up where Emerson left off, seeking inner peace through self-reliance, simplicity, and close contact with nature. What especially set Thoreau apart, however, is that he actually lived in the country. I read that when Emerson and Thoreau visited John Muir, who was the inspiration behind the American national parks movement, Thoreau but not the Bostonian Emerson cared to sleep on the ground at Yosemite with Muir. Thoreau is also the only American writer, I believe, whose words can compete in practical knowledge and depth of wisdom with classic environmental prose in our century by people such as Wendell Berry, who is a knowledgeable row-crop farmer, writer and teacher. Maybe the late Edward Abbey (*Desert Solitaire,* 1968) comes close to Thoreau in audacity of purpose and style.

Before any of these commentators, the ancient Greek agriculturists Pliny and Columella had warned of a human tendency to devalue our relationship with the soil and the creations which spring from it. In areas of China and other Asian countries, centuries-old agricultural traditions are based on concepts with which Henry Thoreau, Seattle, Sitting Bull, Wendell Berry and Aldo Leopold could concur. Until being forced off their lands, many Indian societies practiced large scale but decentralized sustainable agriculture, rotating crops while observing the logic of polyculture and fallowing. Many also knew, according to modern scholars of Indian agriculture, to supply nutrients to the soil with nitrogen-fixing legumes and periodic burning of ground cover.

Meanwhile, Clarence Glacken notes, as the human population became progressively more urban, any landscape by the latter half of the 1800s that presented an attractive scene, no matter the degree of human interference, could qualify as a "pretty place" worth visiting. This appeal particularly extended to the farmscapes between city and the remaining forest, representing a highly mannered leisure-class aesthetic which persists today in densely populated and rapidly suburbanizing farming areas such as, for instance, "Amish country" in southeastern Pennsylvania. Likewise in England, Bunce points out, "the very absence of truly wild landscapes ensured that it would be nature in domesticated settings with which the English would most readily identify. This is reflected in the application of the conventions of the picturesque to the landscaping of country estates in which informal planting and careful arrangement of vistas was intended to achieve the effect of a natural scene. It is reflected also in a shift in romantic art and literature to the celebration of nature in pastoral scenes."

The modern chapter of environmental political philosophy, according to a 1992 book by Bob Pepperman Taylor, may be capsulized in two views of nature's utility: the "pastoral" theories and appreciations represented by Thoreau, and the management of natural resources ethos for which Gifford Pinchot, the infamous Progressive Era secretary of the interior, was the chief spokesman.

An influential historian of ecology, Donald Worster, drew a similar distinction in a widely acclaimed 1977 book, which also correlates the "management" ethos with a distinctly Christian concept of resource exploitation demanded by God. Worster contrasts Thoreau with biologically minded ecologists such as Darwin. He also makes a compelling case for Christianity being the "most insistently anti-natural" of all the major religions. Other scholars, adds Worster, have observed how since the Enlightenment knowledge has required "a strict repression of the viewer's subjective feelings about the object studied. Christianity made this detached, external view of nature possible by overthrowing pagan animism. . . ."

"Romantic" or "idealist" in our age are universal put-downs. Even Thoreau, complains Taylor, never provides "a detailed vision of a society wholly driven by the lessons of nature." I once had a similar opinion of Thoreau, but I can now verify that "nature's lessons," those gained through personal experience, cannot be distilled into a comprehensive guide. By their very nature, such insights are bound to be so personal, spontaneous and potently symbolic that the generalizations required for adaptation to language cannot suffice.

Surely the lesson for anyone prone to pagan daydreams is to speak of them infrequently and in generalities, with carefully chosen company; otherwise one sounds dreamy and pretentious, or kind of deranged.

That's okay, though. The experiencing of nature's chaos makes me prefer that everyone interested be left to it at their own speed, in their own ways.

IN DESCRIBING a mountainscape, though, few knew them or the high meadow tucked within as John Muir did. The world is the better for him having lived near mountains.

A contemporary, John Burroughs, could really write up a fishing trip or a pack of chipmunks he watched; I've had the experience of "coming to" suddenly after several minutes of one of his essays. I read all the modern "nature writers"; I like the subjects. I lived nearly 36 years before discovering Louis Bromfield, and when I found his writings I revisited the wonderment felt earlier for Sir Albert Howard, of early English organic fertilizer fame. I have not found a better blend of farming philosophy with conservationist ideals than Bromfield's. From *Out of the Earth:* "[W]e had not only utilized through organics and moisture the natural fertility of the soil but the . . . moisture and all the other elements including fungi, moulds, bacteria and earthworms which go with a truly living and productive soil in which the eternal cycle of birth, growth, death, decay and rebirth are present."

Just as there is tremendous overlap in the thinking of well-known environmental and nature writers, environmentalism also crosses over frequently with voices in the twentieth century concerned specifically with farming. This is especially true for the 1940s and '50s. Best known is Edward Faulkner, whose *Ploughman's Folly,* a brilliant indictment of 200 years of agriculture with the steel plow, opened the era of "no-till" farming now deployed on an estimated 40 percent of America's farms. Edward Cocanneour's works on soil fertility and the value of weeds are no less excellent. Edward Hyams, with his *Soil and Civilization,* is their counterpart in England and a pioneering viticulturist as well. All flow from the tradition of Samuel Shaler, whom some say was the first to coin the idea of sustainability in farming with his *Man and Earth* in 1904.

Yet, alas, all reviews of such literature in the modern era must end, it seems, with Aldo Leopold. His *A Sand County Almanac* (1947) is widely considered the Bible of American environmentalism. Leopold early in his career was a professional forester with serious sportsman leanings, being one of the first to leave Yale's new degree program in the early 1900s thoroughly inoculated with the professional management ethos formulated by Pinchot. Leopold, working for the U.S. Forestry Service and at the behest of cattle interests, helped direct the eradication of the wolf and puma in the

Southwest during the 1910s, not discovering ecology until the 1930s. He then wrote apologetically about his early career.

Donald Worster has written of a "weakness in Leopold's land ethic that he never really suspected: It was too firmly tied to the science of ecology to escape an economic bias." By the late 1940s, Worster finds, ecologists were sounding like dime-a-dozen boosters, measuring success, as Leopold often did in his essays, in conventional units of "efficiency, productivity, yield, crop." Leopold writes of the "healthy functioning" of the "ecological mechanism," which are lapses, insists Worster, that distance him mightily from the world of Thoreau, for surely Leopold was aware that "organism" and "mechanism" had been identified with "fundamentally antithetical world views" in western discourse for at least three centuries.

Worster makes all of these criticisms in an often powerful book subtitled *A History of Ecological Thought* – meaning "thought" in North America almost completely – and yet he does not devote two consecutive pages out of 504 to Native American civilization or to Native American notions of ecological balance.

Similarly, Roderick Nash, perhaps the foremost American figure in environmental philosophy, contributed an essay on "Leopold's intellectual heritage" in the 1989 *Companion to A Sand County Almanac*. He holds equally high regard for Leopold's ideas but traces them more directly than Worster to Thoreau and Muir. Nash quotes Thoreau (1859) – "What we call wildness is a civilization other than our own" – before adding: "No American had ever thought of anything faintly resembling this before." Overall, I learned from Nash's essay, but no American had ever thought this before? Many of America's aboriginal people, the true Americans, lived for centuries in civilizations based on such concepts.

Esteemed authorities hail Leopold most of all for his insistence on a "land ethic" – "Obligations have no meaning without conscience, and the problem we face is the extension of the social conscience from people to land" – but even before Thoreau, much less Leopold, there was, to name but one society, the Crow. In their view, such a conscience was part of a "sacred trust," and as the term suggests, they suspected it useful for both man and earth, in hunting as in prayer.

Leopold could not have been unaware of Native American contributions to the body of thought on these subjects. In Chapter 6, the 1923 Leopold essay was cited in which he writes that "soil, mountains, rivers, forest, climate, plants, and animals" should be respected "collectively not only as a useful servant but as a living being, vastly less alive than ourselves, but vastly greater than ourselves in time and space." References to time and space recur in countless native religious teachings; they are foundation concepts, simple as they may seem, analogous to Jesus as the savior of all.

Leopold also wrote in 1923 that five cultures have flourished in what is now the United States. "We may truthfully say of our four predecessors that they left the earth alive, undamaged. Is it possibly a proper question for us to consider what the sixth shall say about us?"

But, passed over by twentieth century western commentators just as they were by the Enlightenment, Indian teachers and writers seldom called for large scale rethinkings of the conscious. There is a simple purity in their words that does not fit well with white society's preference for objective detachment and long-windedness.

Primitives, our predecessors on American soil never imagined the needs of people divided from those of the earth. Theirs was a world of blood and flesh, of coyote cousins and bear brothers, and spiritual accumulations. Existence they called "nature."

In the late twentieth century, we have millions who love the wilderness and wish to protect it. Yet, we desperately, desperately need more people who find ways of living from and with that land which is not wilderness, but is where nearly all of us live. Winegrowing is the way I found.

ONE-HALF OF AMERICA'S FAMILIES were not even present when the last Indian exterminations took place. The great waves of southern and eastern European immigration which doubled the U.S. population in roughly three decades took place after the massacre at Wounded Knee (1873).

Yet, the environmental warnings of nineteenth century Indian leaders, and the destruction of Native civilizations, have become part of the American consciousness, and may have much to do with the recent broad revival of interest in ecology and the "Green Revolution" in general. Is there, for instance, a more famous and poignant television ad than the one from the mid-1970s in which an Indian man sees pollution and litter in a stream and a tear comes to his eye? The stereotypical figure essential for effective communication in the mass media about the ruination of our resources was that of an Indian, after all, and not a steelworker or an accountant or even the perennial favorite, a child.

My purpose has not been to argue for recognizing a few Indian tribal leaders as North America's first environmentalists merely because they have been overlooked, or because most scholars consider them apart from John Muir, Aldo Leopold, and (white) others. We hardly need new oppression studies, and besides, achievement is most important for what it teaches.

We also live in an age when huge amounts of natural and human resources are wasted by writers rewording others' arguments. I want to give credit where credit is due; in my research, I learned of J. Donald Hughes, a professor of history at Denver University. After reading his works, I concluded that I did not know enough to even approach the mastery of his *North American Indian Ecology*. So, with his permission, I selected a short excerpt from his book to end this chapter. The numbers for his original citations have been retained here (the citations appear in Appendix iii), so that anyone interested can easily see what I chose to excerpt from his chapter 10.

Then, because Hughes' words help to anchor and to introduce the final portion of what I have to say, his essay continues briefly to begin my next – and last – chapter:

THE DISCOVERY OF THE AMERICAN Indian by environmentally concerned Americans is not entirely new, however. It is quite possible that part of the strength of the conservation-ecology concern is American Indians' presence here and their influence on our national life and thought. Henry Thoreau was fascinated with the Indians, and gave evidence of his study of their personality, culture, and harmony with nature in many pages of his books and journals. "The charm of the Indian to me," he wrote, "is that he stands free and unconstrained in nature, is her inhabitant and not her guest, and wears her easily and gracefully."[3] This is the life style he tried to emulate in *Walden*. In *The Maine Woods*, he speaks at length of his own experiences with Indians, especially his Penobscot guide, Joe Polis, a master of woods lore. John Wesley Powell, not only an explorer but also an influential mid-nineteenth century voice for conservation and reclamation, spent time among the Paiutes recording and preserving their traditions. He translated and published some of their poetry.[4] The Bureau of American Ethnology, which he founded, did more than any other organization to disseminate accurate knowledge about the American Indians. John Muir, the great naturalist, defender of wilderness, and founder of the Sierra Club, often met and talked with Indians. He was adopted by the Stickeen band of the Tlingit tribe and given the name Ancoutahan. He discovered that when he talked to them of his interest in plants, glaciers, and other natural phenomena, he struck a chord of sympathy that the missionaries had never touched. They said they had never heard a white man speak as he did.[5] Listening to an Indian chant, he found that "falling boulders and rushing streams and wind tones caught from rock and tree were in it,"[6] all things that Muir himself loved. "To the Indian mind," he wrote, "all nature was instinct with deity. A Spirit was embodied in every mountain, stream, and waterfall."[7] He noticed their love of flowers and wondered at their knowledge of animals. Indians hold that animals have souls, he noted, and refused to speak disrespectfully of them. One night on a canoe trip toward Chilkat, Alaska, Muir recorded a conversation in which the Indians imputed their own attitudes of conservation to wolves:

> I greatly enjoyed the Indians' camp-fire talk this evening on their ancient customs, how they were taught by their parents the whites came among them, their religion, ideas connected with the next world, the stars, plants, the behavior and language of animals under different circumstances, manner of getting a living, etc. When our talk was interrupted by the howling of a wolf on the opposite side of the strait, Kadachan puzzled the minister with the question, "Have wolves souls?" The Indians believe they are wise creatures who know how to catch seals and salmon by swimming slyly upon them with their heads hidden in a mouthful of grass, hunt deer in company, and always bring forth their young at

the same and most favorable time of the year. I inquired how it was that with enemies so wise and powerful the deer were not all killed. Kadachan replied that wolves knew better than to kill them all and thus cut off their most important food-supply.[8]

Muir said that the Indians' healthy supply of pure air and water is something that "civilized toilers might well envy."[9] His observation of Indians was far too acute to be sentimental, but he sympathized early with the view that "Indians, children of Nature, living on the natural products of the soil" should not be "robbed of their lands and pushed ruthlessly back into narrower and narrower limits by alien races who were cutting off their means of livelihood."[10] Thus Indian-inspired ideas were active in the minds of individuals like Thoreau, Powell, and Muir, who helped to form the conservationist philosophy in America.

Ecological patterns are always changing; the interactions observed today in an ecosystem are the result of other interactions that took place in the past. The subject of ecological studies is never static, and as long as there have been human beings, they have made changes in the natural environment which have in turn reacted to make changes in human cultures. As Robert F. Heizer expressed it, "ecology . . . is a dynamic situation, and its true significance can only be understood in the milieu of time and when analyzed by the historical method."[11] Ecologically speaking, the experience of the American Indians in the natural setting of this continent is the heritage of everyone who lives in North America today. As Vine Deloria says, "In seeking the religious reality behind the American Indian tribal existence, Americans are in fact attempting to come to grips with the land that produced the Indian tribal culture and their vision of community."[12]

-eight-

"*Things that mattered to me once*
won't matter any more,
for I have left the safe shore
where magnificence of art
could suffice my heart."
  – Wendell Berry, "Requiem"

"ONE OF THE INESCAPABLE facts which emerges when we contrast the Indian past with the present is that the American Indians' cultural patterns, based on careful hunting and agriculture carried on according to spiritual perceptions of nature, actually preserved the earth and life on the earth. Since the period of colonization, wasteful destruction of the earth has accelerated. But we cannot convincingly argue that society today should return to Indian ways of life in their entirety; such atavism might be possible for small groups in isolated areas, but not for very many. Hunting and subsistence agriculture could support only a small fraction of our present population. Change is inevitable in all ecological systems, and change is especially rapid in North America today. The question, then, is the direction of change. Shall we continue to move toward ever more destructive use of natural resources, thus making necessary a harsh reckoning with nature and unwelcome constraints on our ways of life? Or shall we direct change as much as possible in the direction of harmony between human beings and the natural environment; toward a state in which we can both use and save, in which we will act with forbearance and nature will provide a sustained yield of renewable and recyclable resources? If we choose the second alternative, we can gain much by studying our American Indian heritage and seeking modern applications of the wisdom we find there. . . .

Perhaps the most important insight which can be gained from the Indian heritage is reverence for the earth and life. Indians did not advance this as a philosophical concept, but developed it by living with nature, depending on its cycles and interacting with the other forms of life. Indian respect for animals was based on observation of their ways within unhindered ecosystems. It springs not from sentiment, but from ethnoscience. Indians had a sense of reciprocity with life, of spiritual resonance with the natural environment, because the biosphere is truly alive and does interact with human beings in ways of its own. . . .

The value of Indian environmental perspectives may lie not in advising a return to earlier ways of subsistence, but in helping to develop a new style of life that incorporates care and reverence for nature and understands the limits that must be placed on human actions and capabilities. One recalls the Navajo chant once more:
May I walk in beauty of abundant rainshowers,
May I walk in beauty of abundant vegetation,
May I walk in beauty;
With beauty before me, I walk,
With beauty behind me, I walk,
With beauty below me, I walk,
With beauty above me, I walk.
It is finished in beauty.[16]

One cannot listen to such a song without feeling that the people who sang it knew that their way was blessed with beauty. There were harsh realities in Indian life, but they were comprehended through the Indians' sense of being in harmony with a surrounding world of spiritual power. Today's life has more physical comforts, but it is not without its own harsh realities. Do we know a path where we, too, can walk in beauty?"

I GREW UP IN THE PROTESTANT faith, and I never remember a minister mentioning god (or Jesus) and concern for any aspect of the natural world outside the church doors in the same breath. I don't actually recall a minister ever making a meaningful mention of the natural world at all.

Not until I read the words of Native Americans did I make a connection between concern for the earth and concern for my ideas about god. And it is in this realm, after all, where the most profound meaning for living dwells.

Concern for the earth and the impact of what I must draw from it is now the spiritual center of a simple personal doctrine that I have pieced together over the last few years of farming wine grapes, making wine, and spending a lot of time in the countryside and in the woods. In addition, I have found that aboriginal people whose cultures I have read about, on many continents, have remarkably related attitudes: that daily life should not be strictly divided between physical and mental existences, and that ultimately, a sense of well-being comes from close personal contact with the earth and its forces.

Donald Hughes noted how "reverence for the earth and life" focuses human energies on the eternally spinning wheel that is existence, and that "Indians did not advance this as a philosophical concept, but developed it by living with nature. . . ." Likewise, the Kogi people of modern Andean Colombia hold that spiritual life and "regular" life in their culture revolve around responsibility to safeguard the "Earth Mother."

A 30-year-old Australian aborigine I saw interviewed on public television gestured to the night sky and said: "Christians want us to pray inside four walls. But I don't need a church. My religion is out here."

I suffer away from the earth. The earth is good to my heart. In many ways, I surely sound like anyone else who has experienced a religious conversion. I try for the words, but I do try not to impose myself overly much. I try to keep it brief.

These Days

THERE WERE OTHER CONVERSIONS as well. I care far less about the grape variety I grow and far less about being the first to make a particular wine from an unusual grape. I want to make wine for a living, but I think the best winery is really a diversified farm business, with wine being only part of what we do and how we live.

We no longer intend to commute to city jobs from a winery. We don't live at our winery property yet (as of this writing, in 1998) but will shortly. We manage the business as best we can on weekends and summer holidays. It's not ideal, but for the present we get the job done.

Our property is less than two hours from our city residence. We found the land in 1996 when we ventured into Garrett County, Maryland, during a camping trip in the Allegheny Mountains. Garrett is a rugged, sub-Alpine mountain county, with elevations up to 3,360 feet – high "tableland country," as the county historian puts it. It abuts Pennsylvania on the north and West Virginia to the south and west.

To capture the spirit of a place in just a few words is tough, but "wild" must be one of them. As late as the mid-1800s, five different sorts of wild cats – including the elusive black leopard of North America, considered by some a temperate latitude variant of the true leopard of the Tropics – and one of the largest bear populations in eastern America roamed the county's glades and valleys. Native Americans are said to have visited from the west in the warm months of the year, hunting buffalo and deer in the grassy meadows and camping in the cool valleys beside the many springs and singing streams. They returned to present-day Ohio to pass a warmer winter. Garrett's cold can be wicked: Oakland, the county seat, claims the lowest temperature (-40°F) ever recorded south of the Mason-Dixon Line; in 1995, some 220 inches of snow fell.

Garrett's modern claim to fame is not well known outside the region: a 100-year-old tourism industry centered for most of the century around Deep Creek Lake. The county has less than 20,000 year-round residents and no large towns but is just three hours from the D.C. beltway.

It also has some of the cleanest, clearest water in the world – one national magazine placed it among the top ten most environmentally pleasant places to live in America – and it also has, we learned in two years, hardworking natives willing to accept equally hard-working strangers. It's an unusual place populated by back-country farm families, truck drivers, and sawmill workers, all a little hard-bitten by the winters, who also have sub-

First vintage, Deep Creek Cellars, 1997.

Wine workers – John and Pauline Grabania –
at Deep Creek Cellars.

stantial contact with wealthy suburbanites that fill the area's motels and condominiums in the warm months. A ski industry provides hearty tourist clientele in the winter, too. Most of the visitors to our winery come from the suburbs surrounding Baltimore and Washington, with Pittsburghers not far behind.

Deep Creek Cellars is a poured concrete rectangle built into the side of a hill – it will double as the foundation for our house – covered with a temporary flat steel roof. I was told one could not buy the necessary winemaking equipment for less than $50,000, but by scavenging and adapting used and less expensive alternatives, we did it for $20,000, made our first commercial wines in the fall of 1997 and opened for sales in July of 1998.

We're two years into it now, and with more than 200 cases of wine sold, I still can't believe it's happening.

Another conversion is that, while I still raise Cynthiana in Pennsylvania, I also grow other wine grapes. At our 2-acre Maryland vineyard, we planted mostly Cabernet Franc, with roughly equal lesser amounts of Chardonnay and red and white French hybrids.

Our growing season is simply too short for Cynthiana, which would ripen there in mid-October, always flirting with frost. We have a very warm site in a cool region at 2,000 feet above sea level on a slope some 800 feet below the summit of Laurel Hill. Laurel is the middle of the three mountain ridges of the Alleghenies that run diagonally across southwestern and south-central Pennsylvania and adjoining parts of Maryland and West Virginia.

Ours is the first winery and the first vineyard in Garrett County, which is generally thought to be too cold for grapes. That's what the Ag Experts say, anyway.

The vineyard faces southwest, and the weather data I collected before deciding to give it a try suggests ours is a warmer growing season than Burgundy but not so warm as Bordeaux. Again, our winters are much colder, with an average of 120 inches of snow each year, but summers are plenty warm with low 80s typical in the day and 50s at night. Low humidity keeps down the fungus diseases.

The soil is rocky and fairly loose, deep but well-drained on the steep slope, which is situated not unlike a ridgeline vineyard in, say, Alsace or Tyrolia. The vineyard rows are planted east-to-west, as in Italy's mountain vineyards – up and down the hills rather than across them, so the sun shines down the row all day long as it advances across the sky.

The steep angle of the sun on our hill really concentrates the heat. We will harvest Cabernet Franc in late September, and Chardonnay before that.

Maybe our vineyard's best natural feature is its stunning view. Visitors are drawn to the top almost magnetically. It seems one can see the curvature of the earth up there; it's almost a 360-degree sweep. We considered putting our home and winery on top of the hill, rather than at the base, but I'm so glad we didn't. Having something built there would have ruined it for the grapes and the other plants – and for those who visit, including us.

In recent years, I've come to especially like the red wines of the Loire Valley from Cab Franc. The aroma reminds some people of mineral-laden raspberries and British wine writer Jancis Robinson, for instance, of pencil shavings. I've also come to value smell as much as flavor in a wine, especially forceful yet refined aromas. There are few things I'd rather do on a long winter night than swirl and sniff a subtle red wine. Aroma sets the stage, and wines with lots of it often end up having a more food-friendly texture. Loire reds are racy and medium-bodied, classic bistro wines, and we will try to make our Cab Franc in a similar easy-drinking style.

This is the style we've picked for our reds in general. Our winery, though isolated, is only 20 minutes from Deep Creek Lake, and wines that can be enjoyed with barbeque on the day they are bought is what the trade demands. Happily, it's the sort of wine that Nadine and I like.

Our first vintage, made from California-grown Carignan and Grenache blended with Cynthiana, was called "delicious and distinctive" by the *Pittsburgh Post-Gazette* wine critic. Artisan Red table wine, as it's called, was received well and we sold almost all of it the first year it was released.

It's a special joy to have a winery in eastern America as a base for making Mediterranean sorts of wines, marrying the two instincts that Ridge's Paul Draper discussed earlier. Our Artisan Red is comparable to a good co-op wine from France's Rousillon. That's Basque country, Catalan and not far from Barcelona, and Carignan does well there. Many people have said our basic red has a Spanish character.

We are very happy to be part of the Maryland wine industry. Having tasted lots of wine from eastern America, I proclaim without reservation that

Maryland's wines consistently are the finest east of the Rocky Mountains. National attention to this fact is slow in coming, but an excellent new guidebook – *Discovering Maryland Wineries*, by Baltimorean Kevin Atticks – will serve as a bugle call.

Carving out an identity in a wine-rich world is the next task for Maryland, and a majority of the state's producers have chosen Cabernet Sauvignon as their top red variety.

Bob Lyon churns out wonderfully distinctive, minty, almost balsamy, Cabernet wines at Catoctin Winery, from vineyards on a renowned fruit-growing ridge by the same name a few miles west of the winery. His wines have a classic mountain-grown character of hefty flavors on a lean mineral-rich frame, not unlike the Cabernets from Diamond Mountain or Randy Dunn in northern Napa Valley. However, Lyon's wines age gracefully, and on a given day one can buy mature Cabernet at Catoctin dating back to the early '80s. He continues a tradition of marvelous Maryland *cru-classé* Catoctin Cab begun nearly three decades ago by the Byrd family.

Still, it's Al Copp at Woodhall Winery, 30 minutes northwest of Baltimore, who is the state's clear Cabernet specialist, with up to a half-dozen blends each vintage of Cabernet from different vineyard sources. Copp shows that Maryland, not Virginia, is the variety's preferred Mid-Atlantic home, for Virginia, like most of California, is really too hot for making wines that resemble traditional Bordeaux. (I like California Cabernet but it's sort of like saying "I like trout" to describe farm-raised trout: there's a "family" resemblance to the genuine item, but my cellar is full of evidence that California Cab, and Virginia Cab for that matter, do not age like the real stuff from Bordeaux.)

Meanwhile, Rob Deford at Boordy Vineyards uses mostly estate-grown fruit for fine Chardonnay that has received recent accolades as the state's "Governor's Cup" wine. It, too, is more like White Burgundy than California Chardonnay, with excellent lychee nut and mineral flavors and great poise. Boordy's entire line is solid. The state's best known winery, and represented on many Mid-Atlantic restaurant wine lists, Boordy is like the Kendall-Jackson of Maryland.

Fiore Vineyards north of Baltimore vinifies up to a dozen wines each year – "The sweet wines pay the bills," explains co-owner Rose Fiore – but the heart of Italian immigrant and trained enogolist Mike Fiore shines the brightest in his dry reds. He makes a lip-smacking good Chambourcin varietal that has zoomed to the top slot in his customers' minds. Estate-bottled, it shows pretty red fruit flavors with a sneaky riptide of spice and chocolate. Anyone familiar with midwestern Chambourcin will see similarities. Fiore is also unusual for producing what must be the only wines from Italianate Sangiovese vines in eastern America.

Yet, I confess a complete weakness for Fiore Chardonnay. It's not oaky, Frenchy, or butterscotchy California. Spinning 'round on delicate pear and guava spokes, it still manages to be hedonistic. It's eclectic and electrifying, similar in an unexpected way to Chardonnay from the cooler parts of Sonoma. I can drink it by the tankerload with lobster or king crab.

To finish this brief tour of Maryland wines, I end with Linganore Wine Cellars. The Aellen family specializes in fruit and grape wines with a dizzying array of fanciful names at affordable prices, and the cars in the parking lot show they have a winning formula.

All of the grapes in Maryland's industry, except for ours, are grown in the eastern third of the state, where all of the other nine wineries are located.

At our property, we also grow and sell Asian pears, with their distinctive crunchy papaya taste, as well as blueberries, raspberries, and even a few vegetables and herbs. In the coming summer, it may be licorice-flavored basil, snap peas, and a couple of oddball lettuces, or something else. We also sell art in our tasting room. In years ahead, we will add chestnuts to the mix and maybe honey and cut flowers, and probably handmade furniture and antiques: diversifications – as well as wine.

Over the vast period of farming's history which predates motorized cultivation, the traditional farmer has been one who spread his labor effectively over the whole year. A successful one, Gene Logsdon of northern Ohio, writes that the "traditional farmer has many, but relatively small, sources of income rather than one or two large sources." This may seem an odd remedy in an age of specialization, of thousand-acre soybean fields. But that sort of farming is not traditional; it's new, only a century old in the human experience. Prosperous farmers whom Logsdon knows sell horses, cows, milk, hogs, honey, eggs, guineas, pigeons, chickens, fruit, ice cream, flowers, collie puppies, cats, and farm tours – all on one farm. "There are even fish in his

The author, new vineyard, 1997.

Nadine after the first vintage, 1997.

horses' water tank."

Logsdon advocates biological efficiencies, letting nature work for the farmer with little human or machine energy. Some simple examples are clover, which, as a cover crop, smothers weeds and supplies nitrogen, or chickens that forage some instead of only being fed grain in closed, small rather than football-field-sized animal confinements, or seeds planted from last year's crop instead of from the farm store. Again, the similarities across cultures among those intent on harmonizing with nature amaze. Masanuba Fukuoka, a tidy farmer of rice and citrus in Japan who wrote *The One-Straw Revolution,* describes a way of farming very much like the one Logsdon practices in Ohio. Fukuoka's reliance on biological efficiency is a pillar in his "lazy farming" – of "letting nature do the work."

Over the very long run, the farmers who endure will reduce or eliminate their use of chemical fertilizers, fungicides, weed-killers, and bug-killers. The total amount of energy expended to mine, manufacture, distribute and apply these farm "inputs" must be brought more in line with the value of the harvested crop. In the industrialized world especially, far more energy is expended to produce a unit of "farm product" than the energy generated by that product after harvest. It costs more to produce our farm products than is derived in benefits. On its face, this is not sustainable.

I am not naive. I know the rub is in who owns and who pays. And the friction will become more pronounced as resources are depleted. Already, if one looks carefully at the terms and their proponents in many clashes over the environment, the argument is really about how long it will be before the strictures of vanishing resources draw blood on the consumer economies of industrialized nations.

Unfortunately, policy-makers and their consultants tend to view ecological threats as isolated challenges. Our governmental system mandates that policy be hammered out mainly in consort with pressure groups, industry, and lobbyists representing narrow notions and constituencies. It's one reason that democracy and capitalism are beautifully suited to an age of ever-expanding possibilities and resources. But imagine a world facing serious shortages of oil and natural gas, and perhaps electricity once the carbon dioxide from burning coal becomes too thick to breath – electric utilities are the biggest polluters in North America today – while we destroy our remaining resources by cutting the boreal and equatorial rain forests (the lungs of the earth) or loose our topsoil to chemical pollution and erosion.

And while the resources dwindle above ground, there is grave concern about the cumulative effects of underground residue from chemicals and fertilizers. It is said to be safe to the environment when Farmer A and Farmers B, C, and D use them according to directions, but the combined effects of drainage from their fields cannot realistically be regulated. As a result, the Tennessee River is "dead" largely because of this cumulative field run-off; vast stretches of the Mississippi River in the upper Midwest are actually hazardous to the touch; large expanses of Chesapeake Bay are being damaged due to nitrate pollution traced to the chicken industry; cancerous chemicals are in municipal water supplies and in water wells across the Corn Belt.

Nonetheless, such threats still have a recognizable face. Through the ages, we see that the biggest danger is human – in our tendency to excess.

This is not the way of a live farmer. He counts on give-and-take with natural pressures. The live farmer may use some chemicals for profitable operation without wanton destruction, but he does so after careful consideration, infrequently, and spaces out such actions when there is no other remedy so that populations of affected organisms may recover and complete their life cycles.

I don't use much insect- and weed-killers, for instance, because I think they are unnecessary in nearly all years to grow grapes on the sites I select. Insecticides popular even in organic farming are deadly to an array of bugs nearly as broad as the despotic DDT. They would kill the grape berry moth, but I avoid the toxins because they would also slaughter the praying mantis, ladybug, spider and other insects which have their own lives – many beneficial to the farmer, to boot – in my vineyard.

Yet, I am not contradiction-free by any stretch: the chemical I use on black rot, though applied sparingly, is similarly "broad spectrum." It wipes out fungal and bacterial agents which are not the fungicide's target. I guess I care more about innocent insects than innocent microbes.

What appalls me even more is the energy I have consumed driving back and forth to my vineyard while living in the city. But only slowly as a city dweller can one work toward a life in the country.

Using sustainable farming techniques, in a polyculture that includes grape-growing, one must not be easily discouraged, tend no more than about 5 acres of grapes, and cleverly market a variety of farm products largely of his own making.

The truism that the fermented beverage is worth far more than the same fruit fresh or as juice has made wine the central product for centuries in small, diversified farms in a dozen European countries. It is a truism that rural policy-makers in America would be wise to ponder, though the subject resides well beyond the boundaries of this book.

But change will not start with government, or in the most ruthlessly capitalized parts of the economic system where profit and shareholder return on investment must be the top priorities. These are the givens in our economic and governmental structure, and though it chews up resources at a shocking rate, the short-term benefits outweigh the detractions. We are, in fact, the envy of much of the planet.

In contrast to previous models that emphasized organizing, networking, media manipulation, and pressure-group tactics, a new paradigm for change, I believe, has emerged. This paradigm recognizes that change will not be revolutionary in tempo – that change can come only over the very long run. It starts in the heart, and it is built one individual on another who chooses today, tomorrow, and next year to do things in ways that are more consonant with the land's needs.

AFTER ALL MY LESSONS, I can see that the reasons most popularly cited for why human beings should want to do their part to improve the ecosystem's health fall into two basic categories: that continuing to degrade the environment is suicidal; and that humans have a moral obligation to allow other animals (and plants, some add) a full life in their native range. Both reasons certainly are sound in themselves.

Yet the step beyond is so simple that I may be excused for having so long feared a trap. I need to live low to the ground, so that I may, upon reflection and retelling by my kind, see every corner of the space I filled and the time it took. If I squander my days distant from the land, then my spirit will suffer. Only in crumbly carbons and all the powers there may I take from the earth my share and see my place in its past with a clearer vision.

Without such a bond, I will be weakened and the lives I touch will be worsened because I cannot give my best to other creations which depend on my active participation. This weakening will not be just a little, though it may not seem a lot.

I believe the path I follow leads to closer contact with the land, and that this is good – always good. Indifference, I am sure, is an unsustainable middle road.

TWO FRIENDS AND A WIFE talk while sprawled in the sun, I see looking over my shoulder, with plenty of flat rock to spare beside a sparkling chute. Their murmurs are all that come to me.

Another friend stands up ahead among boulders along the falls, then wades into the strong current, stiff-legged till waist-deep, and swims around the bend. His splashes reach my eyes silently, drowning in falling water.

The sun is hot, heated wavy air rising from the rocks. In a long absolutely emerald pool, my head a turning speck between flat slabs that form the shore and the waterfalls ahead, I swim languidly; a frog-like crawl. I look at what is. Buff-colored blocks of cliff and boulder, green hemlock and oak, slide by.

The oldest trees on the steepest hillsides in this spot in West Virginia were youngsters a half-thousand years ago. Their parents would have towered here for centuries before. Floods inundating the valley would have altered the stream's course at times, but otherwise, this scene – like a vision of paradise; don't try, you won't find it on a road map – has changed little over the ages.

Indigenous people in the region surely thought this a special place – in all likelihood, as a sign of the Earth Mother's love for worldly creatures. The spot would have taken on what we call a religious significance. In beauty, I am sure, they walked here.

When I look up and down the valley, I think of the Ojibwe Indian's words, "wherever I see her, emotions of pleasure roll in my breast," and, at about the same time, of Henry Thoreau.

"Talk of mysteries!" Thoreau wrote, "– Think of our life in nature, – daily to be shown matter, to come in contact with it, – rocks, trees, wind on the cheeks! the solid earth! the actual world! the common sense!"

I glide on, head turning, puffy clouds at glances. Head to one side as I stroke the green water, I am pleased to see my body is barely a ripple.

With friends, we have come here for years now, two hours down from Pittsburgh on the interstate, and only a few miles south of our winery in the Maryland mountains. I will visit a lot in the future. It's not far at all from where I'll be.

-*appendix i*-

Smalling All Creation by Paul Roberts

In white air on city-hot summer mornings,
I drive alone past others alone hearing
"ozone may harm the ill and elderly."
Expressway windows roll tight,
and downtown, cars heat sky spaces
a rust-colored stink; breathing oil-air
blackens pink-tissued human linings.
Smalling all creation, cities money-dominate.

At the farm, oh sure, tender skins blue to ripen.
But like grape plant, fox, or deer,
I pass whole weeks wind-gulping: whirling, whacking,
woozy to the sun-glob watching.
Pistons clammer, sweat splashes seeing-eye glasses.
Every time I look the plants,
I swear, another foot – exhausting, my body burning.
"Your life-vigor overshadows," I think or sputter.

From field and furrow I rarely wander with nothing pressing.
But Wednesday, walking at woods' edge without my engines,
I noticed, an easy thing, queen anne's lace growing tall up.
Then the kestrel I've known three seasons

came three flaps at canopy,
gliding, gliding, down and down,
down into the bottoms hunting.
A lacewing lands an almond long,
working snail-like a vine leaf dangling I stoop to study.
Lacewing sequined slippers do not blink away.

How to explain?
The kestrel's cry has dinosaurs; a palm of soil every bone.
The delirious-sweet physical – not retreat, nor panacea –
grows one day cherished, a lean addiction from the doing.
Such work and wildness bind the mind to earth's religion.
True, I need and hate the tendons' toil, like some their cities.
But I know I narrow being better in a fairy bug's patience.
Its breath I drink; this pulse on leaf towers with buildings.

-*appendix ii*-

Two Short Garrett Anecdotes (after John Berger)

Buy American
GLENN BAREFOOT is the Native American who owns the auto repair shop on Route 40 above Yough Lake. It's before 9 on a hazy, still summer Saturday morning. I enter a quiet, very cool darkened room with a counter and radiator hoses and automotive what-nots hanging, and a chime sounds. I hear a man – I assume him – talking – I assume on a phone – above me, strangely above me, like in the air. When I listen harder, the sound is more all around than above me. The room is still but time passes very quickly there.

I cannot make out the words, just sounds – "savis-litmus, savis-litmus, savis, uh-huh, litmus" – and I'm looking up in the air and I hear the receiver go down and that "droooor" sound a disconnected line makes, magnified, like on a megaphone, and a man, Glenn, I know it's him because the embroidered name on his shirt says "Glenn," opens the door right beside me and I think I see him slide past and somehow then he is instantly in front of me asking if he can help me and not even blinking, like he may have been there all along. What have I actually seen and heard, I think, is so short a time.

I show him my stripped out steel doohickey. Got anything close? His hair is slicked not too thickly back, trimmed and neat, and he wears greenish matching work clothes of that polyester-cotton material with the nameplate. I smell Dial soap. He's incredibly freshly shaved. Oh yes, he also wears half-glasses, like a professor's, and he takes my hickey and heads back through the shop, messing with it the whole time, head down, a shortish spry man with an economical bent-forward walk, through the darkened bays where cars get pulled in, around a corner and back still more. Many seconds go by, maybe minutes. Still we walk, me behind him. Silence. In one motion he has flipped on a small light above an oily but organized work table, opened a drawer, opened a small case within the drawer, and is comparing my threads to those in the case. His hands move like a surgeon's.

Eight thirty-seconds he mumbles, but, he says, someone has buggered-up his threads on the tap and he fiddles with my thing but can't do anything. Glenn, I ask, do you remember us meeting? He doesn't look up but says yeah I remember you, Deep Creek Cellars, over there off Frazee Ridge Road. Ryder had sent him to repair my rented truck and he had crawled underneath and beat on it with a hammer. If it happens again, he'd suggested, hit it with a hammer and if that don't work, he'd said as he was heading back to his vehicle to leave, me trailing along behind, hit it harder.

You try another bolt? he asks, looking at me. He goes for another drawer and says people work on stuff here and mess up the threads and then put it back in the case and don't tell anyone and then you can't use them when you need to. He digs out a bolt and twists it sternly in. It's strong steel, I see, heavy for so small a piece and highly machined. It's greenish-black but gleams. No, I hadn't, I say, because it was stripped out, but when he hands it to me the new bolt is in real good. There's no waggle to it in the hole.

I screw it in and out and we're walking back to the front and he's saying how for some reason they don't know how to make hardened steel over there and it's just like these foreign tractors or other farm equipment nowadays, they look good and run okay but the metal ain't no good. The comment carries the implication that our stuff is better – and I allow myself to wonder what that must mean to Glenn, whom my neighbors had mentioned was an Indian ("There's more of 'em around here than you'd think.") – and what do I owe you for the bolt, I ask, but he has already handed it to me and just looks at me and sort of shrugs – small, like about eight thirty-seconds of a full shrug – and I look very hard but quickly at his interesting chiseled cheekbones and stoic brown eyes that seem quick to find humour and say thank you several times and I'm heading out the door, which chimes, screwing the bolt in and out of the threads in my soft imported object that some-how were restored by Glenn Barefoot's American bolt.

Horses and Mules Both

ANOTHER MORNING when I came back from Friendsville there was a man standing down by our gate averting the sun with a hand held flat over his eyes, like a scout, looking up our hillside into the vineyard. It was George when I got up to him, and he said quickly with the scantest irony that there is a man walking up there in your vineyard. I turned and saw it was Rick, George's closest friend and our nearest neighbor.

Rick got down to us and there was a little sweat popped out on his fore-head. George and he explained that a farmer had needed to pasture two horses and a mule, and that Rick had the pasture and didn't mind, so the man brought them and they all three right off ran up to the top of the hill. The top of Rick's hill adjoins ours. Directly Rick said the horses came tear-ing down the hill and they could hear the mule up there braying, or, as Rick said, more like just sort of crying, and so he figured he had fallen in a groundhog hole like their other horse had last year (and killed hisself). Or maybe there was a rattlesnake. Or maybe there was a bear, he added, since his wife Belinda seen two and sometimes three bears at a time this year way off up in the field.

But, Rick found out after walking up there that the mule was fine and, he said, was just standing there chewing grass. Horses and mules is both retarded, Rick said, lighting a Winston from the front pocket of his denim shirt which was long-sleeved till he bobbed off the arms right above the elbow. How you doing, he asked me. They's just retarded, he repeated. I laughed, right as George, without the slightest touch of irony, said that it was cause they don't work – neither of them, nope, don't do a thing. A per-son who didn't know him would not know George was being funny.

I realized then his was the driest humor I knew, and what a thing it was to realize, and that Rick and George probably talked like that to each other all the time and I was just finding out.

-appendix iii-

Citations for Excerpt from J. Donald Hughes, North American Indian Ecology *(Texas Western Press, rev. ed., 1998), Used in Chapter 7-8*

[3] Henry Thoreau, *Writings*, Manuscript Edition, 7: 253, quoted in Roy Harvey Pearce, *The Savages of America* (Baltimore: Johns Hopkins Press, 1965), p. 148.

[4] John Wesley Powell, "Sketch of the Mythology of the North American Indians," *First Annual Report of the Bureau of American Ethnology, 1879-80* (Washington, Government Printing Office, 1881), p. 23; see also the original, full text of *Exploration of the Colorado River of the West and Its Tributaries* (Washington, Government Printing Office, 1875).

[5] John Muir, *The Writings of John Muir, Manuscript Edition,* 10 vols. (Boston, Houghton Mifflin, 1916-24), 3: 208-11.

[6] Ibid., 10: 22.

[7] John Muir, *John of the Mountains: The Unpublished Journals of John Muir,* ed. by Linnie Marsh Wolfe (Boston: Houghton Mifflin, 1938), p. 315.

[8] Muir, *Writings,* 3: 151-52.

[9] Ibid., 2: 206.

[10] Ibid., 1: 174-75.

[11] Robert F. Heizer, "Primitive Man as an Ecologic Factor," *Kroeber Anthropological Society Papers* 13 (Berkeley, California, Fall 1975): 2.

[12] Vine Deloria, *God is Red* (New York: Grosset & Dunlap, 1973), p. 88.

[13] Muir, *Writings,* 5:257.

[14] Stewart L. Udall, *The Quiet Crisis* (New York: Holt, Rhinehart and Winston, 1963), p. 17-18.

[15] Charles A. Eastman, *Indian Boyhood* (New York: McClure, Phillips, 1902), p. 3.

[16] Washington Matthews, "Navajo Legends," *American Folklore Society Memoirs* 5 (1897): 275, slightly altered.

-appendix iv-

Producers of Norton & Cynthiana Wines in America

Arkansas

Cowie Wine Cellars	501.963.3990	Marthasville Vineyards	314.433.5859
Post Familie Winery	501.468.2741	Montelle Winery	314.228.4464
Wiederkehr Wine Cellars	501.468.2611	Mount Pleasant Wine Co.	314.482.4419
		Adam Puchta Winery	573.486.5596

Illinois

River Ridge Winery 573.264.3712

Alto Vineyards	618.893.4898	Robler Winery	573.237.3986
GenKota Winery	618.246.9463	St. James Winery	800.280.9463
Owl Creek Vineyard	618.893.2557	Stone Hill Winery	800.909.9463
Pheasant Hollow Winery	618.724.9074	Winery of the Little Hills	314.946.9339
Wing Hill Winery	N/A, 7/99		

New Jersey

Renault Winery 609.965.2111

Indiana

French Lick Winery 812.936.2293

Pennsylvania

Lapic Winery	724.846.2031
Christian W. Klay Winery	724.439.3424

Kansas

Holyfield Winery	913.724.9463
Smoky Hill Vineyards	785.825.2515

Tennessee

Tennessee Valley Winery 423.986.5147

Maryland

Deep Creek Cellars 301.746.4349

West Virginia

Daniel Vineyards	304.252.9750
Jones Cabin Run Vineyards	304.462.5450

Missouri

Augusta Winery	314.228.4301
Blumenhof Winery	314.433.2245
Les Bourgeois Winery	573.698.2133
Heinrichshaus Winery	573.265.5000
Hermannhof Winery	573.486.5959

Virginia

Horton Winery	540.832-7440
Ingleside Plantation & Winery	804.224.8687

-bibliography-

A Note on Other Sources

In addition to the list of books that follow, all of which were mined to greater or less extent for this book, I relied on many magazine and journal articles. Where appropriate, I indicate them in the text. However, in the chapters dealing with Missouri wine history and its early German winegrowers, the sources are too numerous to attribute. The primary sources for those chapters came from the Special Collections Annex in the library system at the University of Missouri-Columbia. In particular, the library's collection of 19th-century midwestern state horticulture association journals and reports and related ephemera were invaluable. I also found the library's run of George Hussman's *Grape Culturist* magazine to be as important to my endeavors as it was to growers in its day.

Books

Edward Abbey, *Desert Solitaire: A Season in the Wilderness* (Simon & Schuster, 1968)

Leon Adams, *The Wines of America* (3rd rev. ed., McGraw Hill, 1985)

Burton Anderson, *Vino: The Wines and Winemakers of Italy* (Atlantic-Little, Brown, 1980)

The Wine Atlas of Italy & Traveler's Guide to the Vineyards (Simon & Schuster, 1990)

Gerald Asher, *On Wine* (Vintage, 1986)

Kevin Atticks, *Discovering Maryland Wineries* (resonant publishing, 1999)

Wendell Berry, *Home Economics* (North Point Press, 1987)

The Unsettling of America: Culture & Agriculture (rev. ed., Sierra Club Books, 1986)

A Continuous Harmony: Essays Cultural and Agricultural (Harcourt, Brace, Johanovich, 1975)

Louis Bromfield, *Out of the Earth* (rev. ed., Aeonian Press, 1976)

Robert Buchanan, *The Culture of the Grape and Wine-making* (Moore, Wilstach &

Baldwin, 1865)

Michael Buller, *In Beaujolais* (Thames and Hudson, 1993)
Four Seasons in Bordeaux (Thames and Hudson, 1991)

Michael Bunce, *The Countryside Ideal: Anglo-American Images of Landscape* (Routledge, 1994)

John Burroughs, *Ways of Nature* (rev. ed., Report Service, 1989)

Michael Busselle, *Discovering the Country Vineyards of France* (Pavillon Books, 1994)

J. Baird Callicott (ed.), *Companion to A Sand County Almanac: Interpretive & Critical Essays* (Univ. of Wisconsin Press, 1987)

Ken Carey, *Flat Rock Journal: A Day in the Ozark Mountains* (Harper San Francisco, 1994)

Ted Casteel, ed., *Oregon Winegrape Grower's Guide* (4th ed., Oregon Winegrowers' Association, 1992)

Oz Clark, *New Classic Wines: Discovering Great Modern Wines, Winemakers and Wine Styles* (Simon & Schuster, 1991)

Joseph A. Cocannouer, *Farming with Nature* (Univ. of Oklahoma Press, 1952)

Joseph A. Cocannouer, *Weeds: Guardians of the Soil* (Univ. of Oklahoma Press, 1954)

Eliot Coleman, *The New Organic Grower* (Chelsea Green, 1989)

Jeff Cox, *From Vines to Wines* (Harper & Row, 1985)

Raymond Dasmann, *The Conservation Alternative* (Wiley, 1975)

David Darlington, *Angels' Visits: An Inquiry into the Mystery of Zinfandel* (Henry Holt, 1991)

Marq de Villiers, *The Heartbreak Grape: A California Winemaker's Search for the Perfect Pinot Noir* (Harper Collins West, 1994)

Hubrecht Duijker, *The Wine Atlas of Spain & Traveler's Guide to the Vineyards* (Simon & Schuster, 1992)

Sarah Jane English, *The Wines of Texas* (4th printing, Eakin Press, 1989)

Barbara Ensrud, *American Vineyards* (Stewart, Tabori & Chang, 1988)

Alan Ereira, *The Elder Brothers: A lost South American people and their message about the fate of the Earth* (Alfred A. Knopf, 1992)

Edward Faulkner, *Ploughman's Folly and a Second Look* (Conservation Classics, 1987)

Édouard Feret, *Bordeaux and Its Wines, Classed by Order of Merit* (3rd English ed., Feret & Fils/Libraires Assoc., 1899)

Jacqueline Friedrich, *A Wine and Food Guide to the Loire* (Henry Holt, 1996)

Masanoba Fukuoka, *The One-Straw Revolution: An Introduction to Natural Farming* (Rodale Press, 1978)

Rosemary George, *French Country Wines* (Faber & Faber, 1987)

Clarence Glacken, *Traces on the Rhodian Shore* (Univ. of Calif. Press, 1967)

David Granatstein, *Reshaping the Bottom Line: On-Farm Strategies for a Sustainable Agriculture* (Land Stewardship Project, 1988)

Leonard Hall, *Stars Upstream* (Univ. of Chicago Press, 1958)

Leonard Hall, *Earth's Song* (Univ. of Missouri Press, 1981)

Anthony Hanson, *Burgundy* (2nd printing; Faber and Faber, 1983)

John Harte, *The Green Fuse* (Univ. of California Press, 1993)

U.P. Hedrick, *Grapes of New York* (State of New York, 1908)
> *Grapes and Wines From Home Vineyards* (Oxford Univ. Press, 1945)
> *A History of Horticulture in America* (Oxford Univ. Press, 1950)
> *The Land of the Crooked Tree* (rev. ed., Wayne St. Univ. Press, 1986)

Eric Hobsbawm, *Industry and Empire* (Penguin, 1968)

Edward Hyams, *Dionysus: A Social History of the Wine Vine* (Macmillan & Co., 1965)
> *Soil and Civilization* (Harper & Row, 1976)

Donald Hughes, *North American Indian Ecology* (Texas Western Press, rev. ed., 1998)

R. Douglas Hurt, *American Agriculture, A Brief History* (Iowa State Univ. Press, 1994)
> *Indian Agriculture in America: Prehistory to the Present* (Univ. Press of Kansas, 1987)

Wes Jackson and Wendell Berry (eds.), *Meeting the Expectations of the Land: Essays in Sustainable Agriculture and Stewardship* (North Point Press, 1984)

Wes Jackson, *New Roots for Agriculture* (Univ. of Nebraska Press, 1989)

Hugh Johnson, *Vintage – The Story of Wine* (S&S Press, 1989)
> *The Vintner's Art: How Great Wines Are Made* [with James Halliday] (S&S Trade, 1994)
> *The Wine Atlas of France and Traveler's Guide to the Vineyards* [and Hubrecht Duijker] (Simon & Schuster, 1987)
> *The World Atlas of Wine* (4th rev. ed., S&S Trade, 1994)

Walter Kamphoefner, *The Westfalians: From Germany to Missouri* (Princeton Univ. Press, 1988)

Aldo Leopold, *A Sand County Almanac* (Oxford Univ. Press, 1947)

Alexis Lichine, *Wines of France* (Knopf, 1962)

Charles Little, *Green Fields Forever: The Conservation Tillage Revolution in America* (Island Press, 1987)

Charles Little (ed.), *Louis Bromfield at Malabar: Writings on Farming and Country Life* (Johns Hopkins Univ. Press, 1988)

Simon Loftus, *Puligny-Montrachet, Journal of a Village in Burgundy* (Knopf, 1993)

Gene Logsdon, *The Contrary Farmer* (rev. ed., 1996)

Leo Loubère, *The Wine Revolution in France – The Twentieth Century* (Princeton Univ. Press, 1990)

Kermit Lynch, *Adventures on the Wine Route* (Farrar, Straus & Giroux, 1988)

Bill McKibben, *The End of Nature* (Random House, 1989)

T.C. McLuhan, *The Way of the Earth: Encounters with Nature in Ancient and Contemporary Thought* (Simon & Schuster, 1994)

Thomas Matthews, *A Village in the Vineyards* (Farrar, Straus & Giroux, 1993)

Oliver Mayo, *The Wines of Australia* (Faber & Faber, 1986)

Mark Miller, *Wine, A Gentleman's Game* (Harper & Row, 1984)

Ted Jordan Meredith, *Northwest Wine: Winegrowing Alchemy Along the Pacific Ring of Fire* (4th ed., Nexus Press, 1990)

Lucie Morton, *A Practical Ampelography* (Comstock Publishing Assoc. [Cornell Univ. Press], 1979)

Winegrowing in Eastern America (Cornell Univ. Press, 1985)

John Muir, *John of the Mountains: The Unpublished Journals of John Muir* (rev. ed., Report Service, 1991)

The Eight Wilderness Discovery Books (Mountaineer Press, 1992)

Roderick Nash, *Wilderness and the American Mind* (Yale Univ. Press, 1967)

George Ordish, *Vineyards in England and Wales* (Faber & Faber, 1977)

Robert Parnes, *Fertile Soil: A Growers Guide to Organic and Inorganic Fertilizers* (Ag Access, 1990)

Emile Peynaud, *Knowing and Making Wine* (English language ed., Wiley, 1984)

Thomas Pinney, *A History of Wine in America: From the Beginnings to Prohibition* (Univ. of California Press, 1989)

Jancis Robinson, *Vines, Grapes and Wines* (Knopf, 1986)

Jan Read, *Rioja* (Sotheby Publications, 1984)

Robert Scheef, *Vintage Missouri, A Guide to Missouri Wineries* (Patrice Press, 1991)

Frank Schoonmaker and Tom Marvel, *American Wines* (Duell, Sloan and Pierce, 1941)

Karl Schwenke, *Successful Small-Scale Farming: An Organic Approach* (Storey Communications, 1991)

Paul Shepard, *Nature and Madness* (Sierra Club Books, 1982)

Richard Smart & Mike Robinson, *Sunlight into Wine: A Handbook for Winegrape Canopy Management* (Winetitles, 1991)

Judith Soule & Jon Piper, *Farming in Nature's Image: An Ecological Approach to Agriculture* (Island Press, 1992)

Joy Sterling, *A Cultivated Life: A Year in a California Vineyard* (Villard Books, 1993)

Jay Stuller and Glen Martin, *Through the Grapevine: The Business of Wine in America* (Wynwood Press, 1989)

Bob Pepperman Taylor, *Our Limits Transgressed: Environmental Political Thought in America* (Univ. Press of Kansas, 1992)

Bob Thompson, *The Wine Atlas of California and the Pacific Northwest* (Simon &

Schuster, 1993)

Peter Tompkins & Christopher Bird, *Secrets of the Soil* (HarperCollins, 1990)

Henry Thoreau, Walden, *Or Life in the Woods* (rev. edition, New American Library, 1960)

Joy Tivy, *Agricultural Ecology* (Halsted Press, 1990)

Roger Voss, *French Regional Wines* (Simon & Schuster, 1987)

Philip Wagner, *American Wines and Wine-Making* (3rd rev. ed., Knopf, 1956)
    A Wine-grower's Guide (2nd rev. ed., Knopf, 1965)

A.J. Winkler, *General Viticulture* (Univ. of California Press, 1965)

Donald Worster, *Nature's Economy: A History of Ecological Ideas* (2nd ed., Cambridge Univ. Press, 1985)

Order Form

Name:_____

Address:_____

_____

City:_____ State:_____ Zip:_____

Phone:_____ E-mail:_____

☐ *Please add my name to your mailing list.*

Please send me:

_____copies of *From this hill, my hand, Cynthiana's Wine* by Paul Roberts $16.95/each

_____copies of *Discovering Maryland Wineries* by Kevin Atticks $9.95/each

_____copies of *Discovering Lake Erie Wineries* by Kevin Atticks $11.95/each

Understand that you may return all books within 30 days for a full refund – no questions asked if books are in good shape.

Shipping:
Please add $1.50 for each book to cover shipping and handling.

Payment:
Cash, checks, and money orders are accepted. Please make checks payable to resonant publishing and send your order to the address listed below.

Send all inquiries to:

resonant ◉ publishing

PMB 179 • 211 E. Lombard St. • Baltimore, MD 21202
info@resonantgroup.com • www.resonantgroup.com